READINGS ON EQUAL EDUCATION
(Formerly *Educating the Disadvantaged*)

READINGS ON EQUAL EDUCATION

Volume 17

EVALUATING THE EFFECTIVENESS OF TITLE I SCHOOLWIDE PROGRAMS:
EVIDENCE FROM THE FIELD

Volume Editors
Diane L. Taylor
Elizabeth A. Kemper

Managing Editor
Pamela S. Angelle

AMS PRESS, INC.
NEW YORK

READINGS ON EQUAL EDUCATION
VOLUME 17
Evaluating the Effectiveness of Title I Schoolwide Programs:
Evidence From the Field

ISSN 0270-1448
Set ISBN 0-404-10100-3
Volume 17 ISBN 0-404-10117-8
Library of Congress Catalog Card Number 77-83137

All AMS Books are printed on acid-free paper that meets the guidelines
for performance and durability of the Committee on Production
Guidelines for Book Longevity of the Council on Library Resources.

AMS PRESS, INC.
56 EAST 13TH STREET
NEW YORK, NY 10003-4686 USA

Manufactured in the United States of America

CONTENTS

VOLUME 17

v

CONTRIBUTOR'S NOTES

KIMBERLEY F. ADKINS is a PhD candidate in education at the University of Chicago. She has been a research assistant for the project "Effects of School Reform on Educational Improvement of Students Considered to be at Risk" since 1997. This research is supported by the Mid-Atlantic Regional Educational Laboratory for Student Success at the Center for Research in Human Development and Education, Temple University. She is currently working at Northeastern University in Boston on a Title II accountability project related to teacher preparation and licensing programs.

PAMELA S. ANGELLE is a doctoral candidate and research assistant at Louisiana State University in the department of Educational Leadership and Research. She has presented her research at regional conferences and serves as managing editor for this volume of *Reading on Equal Education*. Angelle's research interests include induction experiences of beginning teachers and school effectiveness research. She expects to earn her PhD in 2001.

GEOFFREY D. BORMAN (PhD, University of Chicago, 1997) is Associate Research Scientist at the Center for Social Organization of Schools (CSOS) at Johns Hopkins University. He is a principal investigator of several research projects, including "Evaluating the Long-Term Impact of Multiple Summer Interventions of the Reading Skills of Low-Income, Early-Elementary Students," funded by the Smith Richardson Foundation, and of "Title I and Student Achievement: A Reanalysis of the Prospects Data," funded by the Spencer Foundation. Borman is co-editor of a book entitled *Title I: Compensatory Education at the Crossroads*, which will be released during the winter of 2000.

JOAN BUTTRAM is the Executive Vice President and Chief Operating Officer for the Southwest Educational Development Laboratory (SEDL) in Austin, Texas. In this position, she has worked closely with federal and state education officials to design a scope of research and technical assistance activities related to the Comprehensive School Reform Demonstration program. Prior to

vii

coming to SEDL, Buttram served as Director of Research and Evaluation for two other regional laboratories, and as director of an urban northeast school district's testing program. Her work has focused extensively on developing and evaluating programs for low-performing students and districts.

PATRICIA E. CEPERLEY, Senior R & D Specialist, directs applied research projects and develops products at the Regional Educational Laboratory at AEL in Charleston, West Virginia. She recently conducted a research and development project in Cumberland, Virginia, and studied effective and ineffective Title I schoolwide programs. Ceperley is the author of several publications that were funded by the Office of Educational Research and Improvement and published by AEL, including *Standards Implementation Indicators-Charting Your Course to High Achievement*. In addition, Ceperley co-authored "The Impetus for the Tennessee Value-Added Accountability System," a chapter in *Grading Teachers, Grading Schools* edited by J. Millman (Corwin Press).

LESLEY DAHLKEMPER joined Education Commission of the States in Denver in August, 1997, and serves as the ECS/Annenberg Project Manager. Responsible for overseeing work related to a national $6.4 million dollar grant from the Annenberg Foundation, Dahlkemper manages grant activities and strategic planning across all ECS divisions focused on nationwide implementation of comprehensive school reform.

ELIZABETH KEMPER is a postdoctoral fellow at the Center for Social Organization of Schools at Johns Hopkins University. Her research interests focus on school reform implementation and policy issues, specifically their impact upon economically disadvantaged students. She conducts research within the Systemic Supports for School Reform section of the Center for Research on Education for Students Placed at Risk (CRESPAR), including various studies of school improvement models in urban and rural settings.

MARY HELEN S. MCCOY (PhD, Louisiana State University, 1999), formerly a secondary school teacher and administrator, is now with the Louisiana Department of Education where she serves as section administrator for Teacher Certification and Higher Education. McCoy has presented her research at regional and national conferences. Her research interests include teacher standards, teacher recruitment, and issues in secondary education.

THOMASINE HASKINS MENCER received her doctorate at Louisiana State University, where she is an assistant professor in the Department of Curriculum and Instruction. A former elementary school teacher and student teacher supervisor, she currently serves as clinical faculty in the Holmes Elementary Education Graduate Program, and teaches courses in multicultural education. She has presented at state and national conferences. Mencer's research interests include multicultural education issues, professional development schools, and preservice teachers' beliefs and practices.

JAMES MEZA, JR. is Professor and Dean of the College of Education at the University of New Orleans. He is also Director of the University of New Orleans Center for the Accelerated Schools Project (ASP) which provides technical assistance for accelerated schools in the states of Alabama, Louisiana, Mississippi, and Tennessee. He is the representative for ASP on Comprehensive School Reform issues. Meza served previously as the Executive Director of the Louisiana State Board of Elementary and Secondary Education, served as the Interim Commissioner of Education for the State of Louisiana and was a member of the Southern University System Board of Supervisors as Chair of the Academic Affairs and Personnel Committee. His doctorate in education was earned at the University of New Orleans.

SAM STRINGFIELD is a Principal Research Scientist at the Johns Hopkins University Center for The Social Organization of Schools (CSOS). He serves as co-director of the Systemic Supports for School Improvement section of the Center for Research on Education of Students Placed at Risk (CRESPAR). Stringfield is also Co-Director of the Program on Integrated Reform at the University of California at Santa Cruz Center for Research on Education, Diversity and Excellence (CREDE). He is a founding editor of the *Journal of Education of Students Placed at Risk*. As a Kellogg Fellow and later as a member of the International School Effectiveness Research Programme,

Stringfield has studied the politics and economics of school effectiveness and improvement in the U.S., Asia, Africa, and Europe. Stringfield has authored over 100 articles, chapters, and books. His primary areas of interest include school effectiveness and school improvement in high poverty contexts.

DIANNE L. TAYLOR is an Associate Professor of educational leadership at Louisiana State University. She currently serves as President of the Southwest Educational Research Association, and formerly served as secretary for the organization. Her primary research interests are participatory decision making, school reform and improvement, particularly the effects on teaching and learning. Her work is published in several journals, including *Educational Evaluation and Policy Analysis,* the *Journal of School Leadership,* the *Journal of Educational and Psychological Measurement,* and the *Journal of Education for Students Placed at Risk.*

CHARLES TEDDLIE is Professor of Educational Research Methodology in the College of Education at Louisiana State University. He has also served on the faculties of the University of New Orleans and the University of Newcastle (UK) and was Assistant Superintendent for Research and Development at the Louisiana Department of Education. He has authored over 75 chapters and articles and has co-authored and co-edited six books, including *The International Handbook of School Effectiveness Research* (Falmer, 2000) and *Mixed Methodology: Combining Qualitative and Quantitative Approaches* (Sage, 1998). He serves as the series editor for *Readings on Equal Education.*

KENNETH K. WONG is Associate Professor in Education and the Social Sciences at the University of Chicago. He is the author of a recently published book *Funding Public Schools: Politics and Policy.* Currently, he directs a multi-year study on school governance reform in Chicago, funded by the U.S. Department of Education. Together with Dr. Margaret Wang at the Laboratory for Student Success, he co-directs a national study of Title I schoolwide programs.

INTRODUCTION

TITLE I SCHOOLWIDE PROGRAMS: EXAMINING
EVIDENCE FROM THE FIELD

Dianne L. Taylor & Elizabeth A. Kemper

The seventeenth volume of the series *Readings on Equal Education* focuses on Title I schoolwide programs. This volume builds upon a theme established in previous titles in this series, that is, the exploration of federal, state, and local efforts across the United States to ensure that all students have equal and equitable educational opportunities.

Title I originated as part of the 1965 Elementary and Secondary Education Act (ESEA). Its purpose is, and has been, to increase the academic achievement level of low-income youngsters. As Angelle points out in Chapter 4, the program today receives an annual allocation in excess of $7 billion. As one of the most expensive and longest-lived federal education programs, Title I affects almost every school district across the country, whether urban or rural, middle class or low-income. The Title I program, which has been continuously funded since its inception, was slated for Congressional reauthorization in 1999. Lawmakers, however, elected to maintain funding but did not reauthorize the program. Estimates are that Title I will be placed on the Congressional agenda after the 2000 elections.

We have two purposes for undertaking this volume. One is to provide an examination of the strengths and weaknesses of schoolwide programs in advance of Congressional reconsideration of Title I legislation. The second is equally important. This book will add to the small but growing research base regarding Title I schoolwide programs. Many of the contributing authors to this volume describe research they have conducted in schools and/or districts across a number of states. Other authors offer a more comprehensive perspective, examining both the history and the impact of Title I implementation across the county. Together, these studies not only offer a broad perspective for understanding the impact of the Title I program, but also permit comparisons across community context differences.

Organization of the Volume

The volume is divided into three parts. In Part I, an overview of the Title I program from its inception in 1965 to the present is offered. Kemper and Taylor in Chapter 1 provide a historical context for the enactment of the Title I law. In doing so, they trace federal involvement in the country's public schools as it evolved through Title I from primarily an infusion of money into local districts, followed by strict bureaucratic monitoring and enforcement of mandates, and arriving today at a more remote level of involvement tempered by holding districts accountable for outcomes.

Borman, in Chapter 2, adds to the story begun by Kemper and Taylor. He examines the overall effectiveness of Title I, discussing the dearth of large-scale studies and describing trends in the studies that do exist. In addition, he makes a number of recommendations for improving the effectiveness of Title I. Part I concludes with Chapter 3 , by Angelle, who reviews research on pullout programs. She describes the period from the 1970s to the 1990s, when the removal of students from class, or "pullout," was the modal method of providing tutorial assistance to Title I eligible students.

Part II is comprised of four chapters presenting evidence from the field in the form of case studies of successful and unsuccessful schoolwide programs. Taylor and Teddlie, in Chapter 4, compare two schools with relatively successful schoolwide programs, one a "home-grown" program developed by the faculty at the school, and the other a nationally marketed Special Strategy (Stringfield et al., 1997).   In Chapter 5, Wong and Alkins provide a multi-school, multi-state examination of successful efforts using Title I schoolwide programs to implement district reform strategies. They report that while the respective districts promulgated specific improvement plans, flexibility was extended to schools which enabled successful implementation of the schoolwide programs within the context of district improvement efforts.

Ceperley adds a different dimension to book through her investigation of the implementation of schoolwide programs in a rural community. In Chapter 6, she describes a schoolwide program that existed "in name only." Reluctance to give up the pullout model, emphasis on state standards at the expense of effective instructional techniques, and inadequate leadership at the district and school levels contributed to the failure of the program.

Completing Part II is Chapter 7 by McCoy and Mencer. Like Ceperley, they studied schools with ineffectively implemented schoolwide programs. Although their study was of urban schools, they reached conclusions similar to those of Ceperley regarding the importance of school leadership to the implementation of schoolwide programs.

Part III binds this volume together by examining what has been learned through Title I school reform efforts. Meza, Dalkemper, and Buttram discuss in Chapter 8 what has been learned through comprehensive school reform projects, such as those available for implementation through Title I. In addition to emphasizing the importance of leadership at various levels for reform to occur, they also stress the need for targeted professional development based on improvement plan. In Chapter 9, Stringfield reviews the successes that have been made through the Title I program and makes recommendations for the future of the program. Finally, the book concludes with Chapter 10 and an examination of themes which emerged across the chapters in this volume.

Together these chapters present a unique picture of the state of the Title I in the United States. The juxtaposition of a variety of techniques (historical, evaluative, and case studies) used by the authors to present their views, offer the reader an assortment of lenses through which to examine the issues. This volume presents a challenge to both critics and supporters of Title I, by inviting them to view this sometimes controversial program from a variety of perspectives as well as to examine a portion of the evidence for themselves.

Notes

Dr. Kemper's work on this volume was supported in part by a grant from the Office of Educational Research and Improvement, U.S. Department of Education (Grant No. $117D-40005) to the Center for Research on the Education of Students Placed At Risk (CRESPAR). However, any opinions expressed by the author are her own, and do not represent the policies or positions of the US Department of Education.

SECTION I.

History and Overview of Title I

CHAPTER 1

AN HISTORICAL PERSPECTIVE OF TITLE I: TRACING THE EVOLUTION OF THE FEDERAL ROLE IN EDUCATION

Elizabeth A. Kemper & Dianne L. Taylor

Introduction

A cornerstone of the "War on Poverty" reform legislation of the Johnson presidency was the 1965 Elementary and Secondary Education Act (ESEA); the centerpiece of ESEA was Title I. ESEA, in general, and Title I, in particular, were intended to provide an equalizing force among the social classes in the United States by improving the quality of education, especially for children living in poverty. President Johnson was personally committed to this goal of Title I, often referring to education as his own "passport out of poverty" (Johnson, 1965, in Kantor, 1991).

Altruistic as the goal of eliminating poverty was and is, scholars of the period point out that the ESEA also cloaked a hidden agenda. The ESEA legislation was not developed in response to public pressure, nor to demands from educational organizations, nor to cries for aid from state governments. Rather, the driving force behind the ESEA provisions that provide aid to schools attended by poor children, "came from reformers in the Executive Branch who had a double objective: the establishment of the principle of federal aid to schools and a redirection of local priorities" (Murphy, 1991, p. 16).

By expanding the role of the Federal government in public school matters, the Johnson administration entered an arena that had previously been the domain of state and, especially, local government almost exclusively. In entering this arena, Johnson was treading on shaky ground.

Examining the larger context in which the original ESEA legislation was created and the related challenges facing the Johnson administration is one purpose of this chapter. A second purpose is to provide an overview of the evolution of the Title I program across the next three decades. During these 30 years, the focus of Title I has changed from fighting poverty to enforcing procedural compliance, and now to providing a vehicle for promoting school reform. In Chapter 2, Borman continues with a history of the Title I program, examining research concerning the effectiveness of Title I in fulfilling its purpose.

Context of the Original ESEA Legislation

The central thrust of ESEA was to eliminate poverty by improving the education available to poor children. The incorporation of Title I into the Act is symbolic of the political atmosphere during the mid-1960s in Washington. The prevailing view of poverty, which shaped the attitudes of many policy planners at the time, was based on theoretical work by anthropologist Oscar Lewis. Lewis advanced the theory that poverty was based on deficiencies of character found in those who were poor; thus, poverty was a symptom of personal weakness (Patterson, 1981). According to Kantor (1991), the conceptualization of poverty which prevailed in the 1960s can be described as the "culture of poverty thesis." The thesis follows the argument presented below.

1. Poverty stems from the personal weaknesses of poor people, rather than from economic or social conditions.
2. Because poverty is accounted for by personal weaknesses, striving to upgrade the poor, rather than to create jobs or redistribute income, is the best way to eliminate poverty.
3. Concomitantly, because poverty is rooted in a psychological condition, poverty is inherited by children from their parents.
4. Therefore, the elimination of poverty requires professional intervention so that the poor might overcome their inherited

personal weaknesses and acquire skills and attitudes to break the cycle of poverty.

The utilization of such an analysis established a context which allowed for the adoption of a reform, that is, allocating federal monies to local school districts, that focused on "fixable characteristics" and avoided overtly labeling the poor as inherently incompetent. In direct contrast to the post-World War II work programs which created jobs to combat poverty, ESEA sought to change the very nature of those who were poor, thus eliminating the problem at its source.

In addition to this altruistic component of ESEA was the ground breaking, but unspoken, objective of establishing the principal of Federal aid to education. Only rarely before had the federal government encroached on this domain of local rule. Two notable exceptions are the establishment of land grant colleges in the mid-eighteen-hundreds, and the allocation of funds for the development of public school curricula following the *Sputnik* launch by Russia in the late nineteen-fifties. These programs were notable precisely because they were so rare. Previous presidential administrations had tried to enact laws affecting public schools, but had failed. In one respect, prior unsuccessful efforts served as a precedent that increased the difficulty faced by the Johnson administration. But, in another respect, the failure of previous administrations to enact legislation provided a road map of sorts, identifying errors and pitfalls that the Johnson administration needed to avoid. As Kantor (1991) explained,

> [t]he chief task facing those responsible for designing the legislation was to come up with a politically viable bill that avoided the church-state, desegregation, and distribution-formula controversies that had rung the death knell for educational legislation in the past. (p. 60)

The passage of the 1964 Civil Rights Act as well as a Democratic majority in Congress helped to establish a political context in which ESEA could be adopted. To address concerns of critics, the legislation assured state retention of local direction of education by explicitly prohibiting federal control. The law also utilized a variety of reform strategies. For example, ESEA:

- provided support for purchasing textbooks and instructional materials

- authorized the construction of regional educational laboratories to conduct and disseminate basic educational research
- established grants for schools and community groups for innovative educational projects
- provided funding for compensatory elementary and secondary educational programs to assist poor and educationally disadvantaged students.

In spite of attempts to pacify the concerns of various Congressmen, ESEA was not looked upon with general favor by members of Congress. The majority of legislators saw neither a need for such legislation to improve the general welfare, nor a benefit to their constituents. However, by linking education to the demise of poverty, an allocation formula acceptable to the wealthier states was designed which provided funds to almost every Congressional district while ensuring that urban and rural poor children were included as well.

Late 60s and 70s: Putting the Pieces into Place

The ESEA legislation distributed financial resources, the majority of which were linked to Title I, to schools according to the number of poor children enrolled. Confidence was placed in local school boards to determine wise expenditures of monies. ESEA did not specify the types of services that should be provided to "educationally deprived" students, nor did it establish an active role for the United States Office of Education (USOE) with regard to monitoring program implementation.

Prior to the enactment of ESEA, employees of the USOE viewed their responsibility as providing technical assistance to states and local school districts when such support was requested. The USOE had neither the experience of managing grants the size of Title I nor the capacity to step in and administer such a large scale program (Murphy, 1991, Kantor, 1991, Jennings, 2000). In addition, the USOE lacked the personnel necessary to monitor, even superficially, state level implementation of the program. Therefore, as Borman and Angelle point out in Chapters 2 and 3, respectively, the first few years of Title I implementation were fraught with misunderstandings and misapplications of funds.

The results of a 1969 study commissioned by the NAACP revealed that Title I funds were often used for general school purposes. In response to this finding, a comparability requirement was added by the USOE to ensure that the Title I funds were used in addition to, not in lieu of, state and local funding. Although ESEA had an evaluation component built into the original legislation, when Title I was reauthorized in 1974 an additional evaluation component was added to ensure that "objective requirements" were utilized in evaluating Title I implementation.

Throughout the 1970s advocacy organizations such as the Legal Defense Fund lobbied for the creation of more explicit federal legal and regulatory standards to ensure that service to the intended populations would not be sacrificed in favor of more influential constituencies within a school district (Herrington & Orland, 1992). In 1979, the Title I Evaluation and Reporting System (TIERS) was introduced to ensure uniform methods of program evaluation and reporting.

1980s: Formulating Standards and Accountability

With fiscal and implementation procedures of Title I more firmly in place, the focus of Title I shifted to programmatic accountability. During the 1980s, states were required to define levels of academic achievement for Title I students, as well as to identify schools at which students did not show substantial progress toward meeting the desired achievement outcomes.

In 1981, President Reagan tried to repeal ESEA and change the funding formula from categorical assistance into block grants given to each state, with few strings attached to define how the funds would be used. Reagan failed, and in 1982 the Education Consolidation Improvement Act (ECIA) reauthorized ESEA and Title I. The 1982 legislation also consolidated funding to address state-level concerns related to administering federal categorical programs and the accompanying reporting procedures (Alexander & Soloman, 1996). However, the cut back in federal funding to Title I during the Reagan years was so severe "that it took ten years for the number of students being assisted to be restored to 1980 levels" (Jennings, 2000).

Title I was again reauthorized in 1988 and amended to require states to define levels of academic achievement for Title I students, and to identify those schools at which students did not show substantial progress toward meeting desired achievement outcomes. The 1988 Hawkins-Stafford Amendments established

steps that districts and states had to follow to assist low-performing Title I schools, beginning with school developed improvement
plans and progressing to state intervention with consistently low-
performing schools (Le Tendre, 1991; Timar, 1994).   Another
important element of the 1988 Hawkins- Stafford Amendment
was loosening the requirements that funds be spent exclusively on
"Title I eligible" students.   Instead Title I funds were made
available for schoolwide projects. These changes in the law laid
a foundation for the federal government to apply pressure on
schools to improve the quality of education provided, rather than
pressure to account for expenditures.

1990s: School Standards and School Wide Projects

The 1990s saw another change in the focus of the Title I
program.   At the school level the response to the Hawkins-
Stafford Amendments was slow. Schools were reticent to adopt
schoolwide programs, both because of uncertainty regarding
federal intent, and because of restrictions in the amendments
related to implementation of schoolwide programs. However, as
the decade progressed, the shift in emphasis from fiscal and
programmatic compliance to educational improvement through
schoolwide implementation grew. Foreshadowing the beginning
of a new emphasis on standards was the introduction of "America
2000" by President Bush, a program advocating national academic
standards and testing.
In 1994, Congress passed the Improving America's Schools
Act (IASA) which reauthorized the Title I program. As part of the
reauthorizaton, IASA required states to develop academic
standards, to define levels of student mastery, and to assess
student achievement. The main impact of this reauthorization
was in the following five areas (Billig, 1996):
1. Increased the flexibility of Title I in program design and
delivery to encourage innovation.
2. Mandated that all children be held to the same challenging academic standards.
3. Targeted funds to areas of greatest need.
4. Encouraged family and community partnerships with the
focus on helping all children succeed.

5. Encouraged development of support systems to assist school level practitioners to design, deliver, and improve programs for and services to all students.

In addition, the 1994 reauthorization was specifically amended so that "pull-out" programs could be replaced with schoolwide programs. Pull-out programs were initially designed to meet the strict accountability requirements of the 1974 reauthorization of the program. As Angelle explains in Chapter 3, these provisions mandated that local districts be able to demonstrate that monies were spent directly on services for "eligible" children. However, complaints from educators mounted over the years about the disruptive nature of the pullout model. At the same time, evidence accumulated indicating that the emphasis in the pullout classroom was on basic skills at the expense of thinking skills. As a result, legislators were persuaded to ease requirements for schoolwide programs when Title I was reauthorized through IASA. Under the new formula, schools could qualify for schoolwide projects if at least 50% of the student body was from low-income families.

Building upon the theme of establishing high academic standards for all students, in 1997 the Obey-Porter legislation initiated the Comprehensive School Reform Demonstration (CSRD) program. As Meza, Dahlkemper, and Buttram point out in Chapter 8 of this volume, this federally funded program provides financial incentives to schools, especially Title I schools, to support the implementation of schoolwide research-based initiatives to raise student achievement. The focus of the CSRD program is the utilization of "proven practices" to insure the academic success of all students.

Conclusion

ESEA was a groundbreaking piece of legislation. It institutionalized the role of the federal government in providing education to poor children. ESEA, and specifically Title I, is unique in its aim to eliminate poverty through education. In short, ESEA re-emphasized the importance of education as a primary vehicle for social change.

As detailed in Table 1, ESEA and subsequent legislation tied to its reauthorization has transformed the original focus of the legislation from fighting poverty to focusing on whole school reform, particularly schools attended by poor children. The conflict over Title I has always been between the traditionalists who want general aid to education and reformers who want schools to do more and perform better for disadvantaged children.

Table 1. Title I Time Line.

1965	ESEA enacted
1969	NAACP study revealed that funds were often used for general school purposes. USOE adds a comparability requirement to ensure that funds were used in addition to, not in lieu of, state and local funding
1974	Title I reauthorized, an evaluation component added into the legislation to ensure that "objective requirements" were utilized in evaluating Title I implementation.
1979	Title I Evaluation and Reporting System (TIERS) introduced to ensure uniform methods of program evaluation and reporting.
1981	Title I reauthorized under the Educational Consolidation and Improvement Act (ECIA), in spite of attempts to repeal ESEA and transform the compensatory education monies into block grants to states.
1988	Title I reauthorized and amended to require states to define levels of academic achievement for Title I students, and to identify those schools whose students did not show substantial progress toward meeting desired achievement outcomes.
1991	President Bush introduced America 2000, a program for national academic standards and tests.

1994	Improving America's School Act, reauthorized Title I. Required states receiving funds to have academic standards, to define levels of student mastery, and to assess student achievement. Requirements for schoolwide programs were eased so that schools could qualify if at least 50% of the student body was from low-income families.
1997	Obey-Porter legislation established the Comprehensive School Reform Demonstration program.
1999	Educational Excellence for All Children Act, attempted to reauthorize Title I, but did not pass.

As we end the year 2000 the future of ESEA has yet to be decided. Although President Clinton presented the Educational Excellence For All Children Act in 1999, neither his version nor any of the Republican proposals for reauthorization have passed Congress as of this writing (funding for Title I at its current level has been approved without legislative reauthorization of the program). Critics of ESEA would like to see the next reauthorization transform the monies into block grants and vouchers to give power directly to the states and individual families (Finn & Petrilli, 1998). Proponents of the program, on the other hand, would like to ensure that the focus of the funding remains on economically disadvantaged students (Jennings, 2000). As we enter the new millennium it will be interesting to continue to trace the evolution of ESEA, and the changing role of the United States federal government in education.

References

Alexander, K. & Salmon, R. G. (1995). *Public School Finance*. Boston: Allan and Bacon.

Billig, S. H. (1998). Implementation of Title I of the Improving America's Schools Act: A 1997-98 update. *Journal of Education for Students Placed at Risk, 3* (3), 209-222.

Cohen, D. K. (1982). Policy and organization: The impact of state and federal educational policy on school governance. *Harvard Educational Review, 52*(4), 474-499.

Finn, C. E. Jr. & Petrillit, M. J. (1998). Washington vs. school reform. *The Public Interest, Fall* (133), 55-68.

Heid, C. A. (1991). The dilemma of Chapter I program improvement. *Educational Evaluation and Policy Analysis, 13* (4), 394-398.

Jennings, J. F. (1991). Chapter I: A view from Congress. *Educational Evaluation and Policy Analysis, 13*(4), 335-338.

Jennings, J. F. (2000). Title I: Its legislative history and promise. *Phi Delta Kappan, 81* (7) 516-522.

Herrington, C. D. & Orland, M. E. (1992). Politics and federal aid to urban school systems: The case of Chapter One. In J. G. Cibulka, R. J. Reed, & K. K. Wong (Eds.). *The politics of urban education in the United States: The 1991 yearbook of the Politics of Education Association.* Washington, D.C.: Falmer Press, 167-179.

Kantor, H. (1991). Education, social reform, and the state: ESEA and federal education policy in the 1960s. *American Journal of Education, 100* (1), 47-83.

Kirst, M., & Jung, R. (1991). The utility of a longitudinal approach in assessing implementation: A thirteen year view of Title I, ESEA (pp. 139-163). In A. R. Odden (Ed.). *Education Policy Implementation.* Albany, New York: State University of New York Press.

LeTendre, M. J. (1991). The continuing evolution of a federal role in compensatory education. *Educational Evaluation and Policy Analysis, 13*(4), 328-334.

Murphy, J. T. (1991). Title I of ESEA (pp. 13-38). In A. R. Odden (Ed.). *Education Policy Implementation.* Albany, New York: State University of New York Press.

Patterson, J. T. (1981). *America's struggle against poverty, 1900-1980.* Cambridge, Massachusetts: Harvard University Press.

Timar, T. (1994). Federal education policy and practice: Building organizational capacity through Chapter 1. *Educational Evaluation and Policy Analysis, 16*(1), 51-66.

CHAPTER 2

THE OVERALL EFFECTIVENESS OF TITLE I:
A REVIEW OF RECENT RESEARCH

Geoffrey D. Borman

Introduction

Since the inception of Title I, research and evaluation have been important elements of the program. Title I was the first federal education law to mandate annual effectiveness evaluations (Timpane, 1976). In addition, the federal government has sponsored two national evaluations and a number of smaller studies that have contributed to the Title I research base. More recently, significant efforts by researchers at the Center for Research on the Education for Students Placed At Risk (CRESPAR) and their colleagues have focused on a quantitative synthesis of three decades of Title I evaluation research and on a series of analyses of the recently collected Prospects and Special Strategies data. This work, along with other research, is described in greater detail in a forthcoming volume, *Title I: Compensatory Education at the Crossroads* (Borman, Stringfield, & Slavin, in press). In this chapter, I summarize the ways in which this recent research informs two questions: (1) what is the overall effectiveness of Title I; and (2) how can it become a more effective program? I conclude with three recommendations to foster better research and better programs: (1) implement a uniform, national accountability system to replace the discontinued Title I Evaluation and Reporting System (TIERS); (2) support continued

11

development and formative evaluation of programs and methods for improving schooling for disadvantaged children; and (3) encourage statewide randomized experiments of promising programs and practices.

The Overall Effectiveness of Title I

The overall effectiveness of an educational program may be evaluated by various means. Two of the most important standards are: (a) is the treatment implemented; and (b) is it producing the intended changes in relevant outcomes? As many researchers have demonstrated, if an educational intervention is poorly implemented, understandably, it will have little impact on those who are served by it (Berman & McLaughlin, 1977; 1979; Crandall, et al., 1982; Stringfield, et al., 1997). Since the beginning of Title I, the matter of implementation has been a key concern of federal policymakers, and has played a great role in shaping the development and effectiveness of the program over the 35 years of its existence. Although the question of program impact seems straightforward, the intended changes, and how those changes are measured, have been defined in varying ways. These differing definitions have resulted in contrasting perspectives on Title I's overall effectiveness. As I discuss below, a review of the historical evidence of Title I effectiveness, as measured against these two standards, provides a strong sense of the evolution and current status of America's most significant effort to improve education for at-risk students. This review of the evidence, which is provided in greater detail in Borman and D'Agostino (1996; in press), incorporates evaluation data collected from 1966 to 1993, and includes the test scores of over 41 million Title I students.

Implementation

Borman and D'Agostino's (1996) review of the Title I research literature suggested that the main value of the early federal evaluations was in addressing the most basic standard of implementation. These studies asked the question: "Were the federal funds being spent on the targeted students for the intended purpose of providing some form of supplemental educational services? Research sponsored by the Washington Research Project and the NAACP Legal Defense and Educational Fund provided one of the more prominent reports of large-scale violations in the operation of the program (Martin & McClure, 1970). Similarly, Wargo, Tallmadge, Lipe, and Morris (1972) concluded that localities disregarded regulations, guidelines, and program criteria, and had not implemented Title I as intended by Congress.

Poor implementation during the early years of Title I may be traced to several political, economic, and practical problems. Perhaps naively, federal policymakers assumed that "once the public school system received the dollars it craved, it would reform from within and reach out to poor children whom it had neglected for so long" (Jeffrey, 1978, p. 136). However, the early operation of Title I proved to be a disappointing commentary on the possibilities of local control. Many districts and schools were found to use Title I funds as general aid, spreading resources widely rather than targeting them on disadvantaged children. This outcome is, in part, explained by the tension between local policies, which tend to emphasize economic productivity, and federal policies, which reflect a relatively greater concern for equality. Federal programs, such as Title I, which are designed to redistribute funds to benefit needy and unfortunate populations, are not easily implemented by local governments because they negatively affect local economies and conflict with the economic self-interests of communities (Peterson, 1981). Senator Robert Kennedy, who was convinced that local school systems would be obstacles to implementing the equality-minded ESEA legislation, testified before the Congress: "If you are placing or putting money into a school system which itself creates this problem [of inequality], or helps create it, or does nothing, or little, to alleviate it, are we not just in fact wasting the money of the federal government?" (Jeffrey, 1978, p. 85).

In addition to the conflicts between federal goals of equality and local economic self-interests, McLaughlin (1976) cited other reasons for noncompliance. First, the original program mandates were ambiguous concerning the proper and improper uses of Title I funds, and the guidelines and intent of the law were open to varying interpretations. Some local officials considered Title I as a general aid fund, which masqueraded as a categorical funding source for diplomatic and political reasons only. The "proper" use of the federal funds depended upon local interpretation. Second, in 1965 the educational knowledge base for developing effective compensatory education programs was extremely limited. Therefore, the majority of local administrators and teachers lacked the experience and understanding for developing, implementing, and teaching compensatory programs. Third, although the federal dollars provided localities an incentive to improve education for the disadvantaged, a viable intergovernmental compliance system was not in place. Without effective regulation, the receipt of funds did not depend on meeting the letter or the spirit of the law. Responding to local self-interests, and utilizing Title I dollars for established general aid policies, was an easier option than the new and more complicated task of implementing effective programs for poor, low-achieving students.

Despite early resistance by most federal policymakers to restrict local control, the findings of Martin and McClure's (1969) study, and the pressures exerted by growing numbers of local poverty and community action groups, prompted the U.S. Office of Education to reconsider the legislative and administrative structure of Title I (Jeffrey, 1978; Kirst & Jung, 1982). During the 1970s, the Congress and U.S. Office of Education established more prescriptive regulations related to school and student selection for services, the specific content of programs, and program evaluation, among other things (Herrington & Orland, 1992). Furthermore, the Office of Education took steps to recover misallocated funds from several states, and warned all states and localities that future mismanagement would not be tolerated. These additional legal responsibilities placed greater administrative demands on local school systems. Funded in part by federal dollars, larger and more specialized state and district bureaucracies emerged to monitor local compliance. State and local compliance was confirmed through periodic site visits and program audits by the U.S. Office of Education and by the Department of Health, Education, and Welfare. As Cohen (1982) and Meyer, Scott, and Strang (1986) noted, the Title I legislation of the 1970s, along with the proliferation of other state and federal educational mandates, promoted the expansion and increased bureaucratization of local educational agencies.

As the 1970s progressed, the bureaucratic organization of Title I became institutionalized across the country and services were delivered to the children targeted by the law (Peterson, Rabe, & Wong, 1986). Rather than a heavy federal presence and intergovernmental conflict, the implementation of Title I became a cooperative concern and professional responsibility of local, state, and federal administrators. In addition, Peterson and his colleagues noted that Title I had inspired greater local concern for, and attention to, the educational needs of the children of poverty. Therefore, in marked contrast to the first decade of the program, during the latter half of the 1970s and throughout the 1980s the specific legislative intents, and the desired hortatory effects, were achieved on a far more consistent basis.

After this basic standard of implementation was achieved, during the late 1980s and throughout the 1990s, new legislation contained in the Hawkins-Stafford Amendments of 1988 and the Improving America's Schools Act (IASA) of 1994 focused on reforming and improving services in Title I schools. This new legislation offered schools greater latitude in designing and implementing effective programs, but also included new provisions that held them accountable for improved student outcomes and designated a program improvement process for those schools with poor or declining performance. The law encouraged frequent and regular coordination of the Title I program with the regular classroom. Also, all schools with high concentrations of poverty became eligible to use their Title I funds for schoolwide projects to upgrade the school as a whole. Rather than fiscal and procedural accountability, more recently, Title I policymakers have attempted to craft laws encouraging, and to some degree mandating, accountability for reform and improvement.

Although these new policies appear to be steps in the right direction, there is mixed evidence concerning the impact they have had on the quality of services. After the 1988 reauthorization, observers noted that the legislation did not alter the general organizational structure of Title I and had a limited impact on the established priorities of its administrative network. Matters of compliance rather than coordination and improvement of services continued as central administrative priorities. For instance, Herrington and Orland's (1992) study of four urban districts during 1990 documented no dramatic changes in local policies, administrative structures, and service delivery arrangements. Similarly, based on visits to nine state educational agencies and some of the districts they served, Millsap, Turnbull, Moss, Brigham, Gamse, and Marks (1992) concluded that despite the dedication of Title I administrators, they had a limited role in advancing the new program improvement goals. Administrators indicated three common obstacles to increased involvement in Title I improvement: small staffs; the burden of other traditional responsibilities; and the fact that staff members tended to be more comfortable dealing with fiscal and compliance issues than with curricular and instructional matters.

The 1994 reauthorization of Title I and current discussion regarding the future federal role in the nation's schools have been influenced by the national education goals, which exhort "world class" standards of academic performance for *all* students, and by a "systemic" approach to reform in which state and local education systems change incompatible policies and objectives in coherent and coordinated ways to produce improved educational processes and outcomes (Orland, 1994). Recently, though, the Citizens' Commission on Civil Rights (1998) issued a report stating that the implementation of the new provisions has been slow and uneven. The Commission concluded that the U.S. Department of Education has been reluctant to take the actions needed to implement and to enforce the new Title I requirements. Because of this reluctance, the Commission reported that many state and local education officials have received the impression that the new Title I law is essentially a deregulation law designed to free them from bothersome federal conditions, and have failed to understand that the tradeoff in the law is higher standards and accountability for results. Other recent reports provide a more optimistic picture, indicating that states and urban school systems have made significant progress in developing the new accountability provisions (Council of the Great City Schools, 1999; U.S. Department of Education, 1999), and that schools are making better use of program delivery models that integrate Title I with the regular academic program (U.S. Department of Education, 1999). Similar to the situation after the 1988 reauthorization, though, it seems most states lack the capacity to assist Title I schools in need of reform and improvement (U.S. Department of Education, 1999).

Is Title I Producing the Intended Changes?

The primary goal of Title I is to eradicate, or to significantly narrow, the achievement gap separating educationally and economically disadvantaged children and their more advantaged peers. For a program as large and long-lived as Title I, though, there is surprisingly little high quality, systematic evidence to assess how well it has accomplished this goal. Withholding services from eligible students would not generally be legal, and, thus, no random experiment of Title I effects has been conducted. Therefore, most evaluations using control groups have employed quasi-experimental methods with differing control-group definitions and criteria.

The goal of "closing the achievement gap" has two distinct definitions that have influenced the selection of an appropriate quasi-experimental control group (Borman & D'Agostino, 1996). Some researchers have attempted to respond to the question: does participation in Title I narrow the achievement difference between program participants and the nation's more advantaged students? Others have questioned whether this gap would widen without the existence of Title I services. Researchers have responded to the former question by comparing Title I students to all non-participating students, while the latter question has been addressed by comparing Title I students to similarly needy controls who did not receive compensatory education services. However, these types of comparisons are very rare at the local level and have been implemented in only two nationally representative assessments of the program: the Sustaining Effects Study and the Prospects evaluation. The vast majority of evaluations of Title I programs has been based on pre-post change scores from various norm-referenced achievement tests administered on either a fall-to-spring or annual testing cycle. According to the norm-referenced model, if the mean change score of participating students within a school is greater than 0 normal curve equivalents (NCEs), which are normalized percentile scores with a mean of 50 and a standard deviation of 21.06, the program is said to be effective. A mean gain greater than 0 NCEs has been interpreted as evidence of programmatic impact, on the assumption that in the absence of Title I intervention students tend to remain at the same national percentile rank over time – the "equipercentile assumption" (Tallmadge & Wood, 1981).

As Borman and D'Agostino (1996) documented, the choice of the evaluation model has a significant impact on the results and on the interpretation of the program's effects. Also, because Title I remains essentially a funding source rather than a specific programmatic intervention, differences in the ways schools implement the program affect estimates of its effectiveness. For these reasons, Borman and D'Agostino's meta-analysis of Title I and student achievement indicated that, from a statistical standpoint, the overall program effect is most appropriately conceived of as random. In other words, although the overall weighted, mean Title I effect size of $d = .11$ (or an average yearly achievement gain of 2.3 NCEs) is significantly greater than 0, it is not extremely meaningful because the estimates of effectiveness are highly dependent on the widely varying ways in which services have been evaluated and implemented over the years. For instance, with regard to differing evaluation techniques, Borman and D'Agostino's analysis indicated that quasi-experimental control group comparisons tend to yield more conservative effect estimates than do norm-referenced comparisons. Also, primarily due to the deleterious effects of summer vacations on student achievement (see Cooper, Nye, Charlton, Lindsay, & Greathouse, 1996; Heyns, 1978), evaluations of norm-referenced achievement gains over an annual testing cycle tend to result in more conservative effect estimates than do evaluations that are restricted to school-year, or fall-to-spring, achievement gains.[1] The grade and subject supported by Title I also influence effect estimates, with programs in reading and programs in middle and high schools showing less evidence of effectiveness than, respectively, math and elementary school programs.

In addition to these statistical main effects, Borman and D'Agostino (1996) found several interaction effects of note. First, contrary to the claims of previous Title I researchers, the interactions of subject and testing cycle, and grade level and testing cycle influence the interpretation of the grade and subject main effects. Consistent with the meta-analysis of summer learning by Cooper et al. (1996), the subject-by-testing-cycle interaction reveals that students' math achievement suffers to a greater extent than their reading achievement due to the intervening summer months. Also consistent with Cooper et al., the interaction between testing cycle and grade suggests that the summer effect is more deleterious to at-risk students in the intermediate and upper grades. The substantially smaller annual gains for math students and for middle and high school students suggest that Title I interventions during the regular school year alone may not sustain their relatively large fall-to-spring achievement improvements.

Also in contrast to the review by Kennedy, Birman, and Demaline (1986), which suggested that math program participants consistently outperform reading participants across all grades, the subject-by-grade interaction reveals a different pattern. Math

participants from grades 1 through 6 hold a considerable achievement gain advantage relative to reading participants, but this
advantage virtually disappears from grades 7 through 12. This
pattern suggests that the effect of Title I math programs is
especially powerful during the initial years of schooling. Other
work by Borman, Wong, Hedges, and D'Agostino (in press)
provides one possible explanation for this phenomenon. Borman
and his colleagues found that regular classroom teachers in the
elementary grades devote an average of about 7.5 hours per week
to Title I students' reading/language arts instruction, but spend
only about 3 hours per week on math instruction. Because
elementary students spend relatively similar amounts of time in
supplemental Title I reading/language arts and math programs, and
considerably less time in regular classroom math than reading
settings, Title I math programs have a much more pronounced
relative effect on students' total math learning time. In middle and
high schools, though, there is far less discrepancy between the
time students spend in self-contained math and reading/English/
language arts classes.

Most importantly though, and related to the previous
discussion of the history of Title I's implementation, Borman and
D'Agostino (1996) found that the effects of Title I have improved
significantly over the life of the program. After controlling for all
the significant moderators of Title I effects, except for year of
implementation, Borman and D'Agostino (in press) obtained the
residuals from the regression. Because the residuals have an
average of 0, the researchers used a procedure called "fitting an
average value to the regression," which added the average
unweighted effect size, $d = .12$, to each residual. Figure 1, a
scatterplot of adjusted effect size by year of implementation,
provides a visual representation of how Title I effects have
changed over the years, after statistically controlling for all of the
other moderator variables discussed above.

The figure contains 657 data points, each representing an
independent estimate of the Title I effect derived from 17 national
studies and including the test scores of over 41 million Title I
students. The line of best fit through the data points indicates a
somewhat non-linear relationship between adjusted effect size and
year of implementation. Specifically, Figure 1 shows a linear
improvement in program effects from 1966 to the early 1980s,
increasing from an effect size of about 0 in 1966 to an effect of

<u>Figure 1.</u> Scatterplot of adjusted effect size by year of Title I implementation.

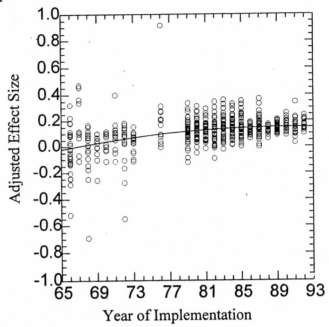

Year of Implementation

nearly .15 in the early 1980s. This suggests that when localities implemented programs of variable, but generally poor, quality, during the 1960s the effects were, on average, essentially zero. Improved implementation led to improvements in the effectiveness of the program during the 1970s. However, beginning in the 1980s the effects plateaued, remaining at around .15 throughout most of the 1980s and the early 1990s.[2] This pattern of improvement in Title I effects suggests that once the program was effectively implemented as intended by Congress during the late 1970s and early 1980s, the effects reached a peak that has not changed substantially. The pattern of variability in program effects also supports this conclusion. The wide variation in program effects during the 1960s and early 1970s appears to reflect the variability of local program implementation and evaluation. However, once implementation and accountability requirements became more uniform and established throughout the late 1970s and 1980s, this not only led to increased effectiveness, but to more consistent effectiveness. One may conclude that this result could be read to suggest that an effect of .15 is the best we can do given the current federal funding commitment. Alternatively, it could be taken as a sign that the standardized, and modestly effective, procedures of the past 20 years require substantial reform in order to promote continued improvement.

Although an overall, fixed Title I population effect estimate cannot be determined from existing federal data, from a summative perspective the program appears to have contributed to the achievement growth of the children it has served. During the 1960s and early 1970s, Title I was not regarded as an effective program primarily because localities did not implement it as intended by Congress (see McLaughlin, 1977; Rossi, McLaughlin, Campbell, & Everett, 1977; Wargo et al., 1972). However, the positive trend of the program's impact suggests that as the U.S. Department of Education and Congress have taken the initiative to develop more stringent implementation and accountability standards, Title I has evolved into a more viable and effective intervention. The evidence from Title I evaluations indicates that the program has not fulfilled its original expectation: to close the achievement gap between at-risk students and their more advantaged peers. The results do suggest, though, that without the program children served over the last 30 years would have fallen farther behind academically.

Improving the Effectiveness of Title I

Once a basic level of program implementation was widely attained, policymakers and researchers began to focus their efforts on program improvement. With the most recent reauthorization of Title I in 1994, these efforts have intensified. During this new era of Title I, program improvement is increasingly viewed as a process of implementing research-proven programs and practices. The Comprehensive School Reform Demonstration Program (CSRD) is one prominent example of recent federal legislation aimed at Title I schools to encourage large-scale implementation of programs with a solid research base. Through CSRD, Title I schools (and some non-Title I schools) may apply for additional funding for start-up implementation of a comprehensive model to reform and upgrade the entire school program.[3] One of the foremost criteria in approving the applications for CSRD funding is that the model proposed for implementation is one with a strong research-proven record of effectiveness. Most models are developed by groups external to the schools, such as universities and educational centers and labs. In a number of cases, these models have undergone years, or even decades, of design, development, evaluation, and refinement. Therefore, state and local education agencies, which have generally lacked the organizational capacity and funding to develop and to help implement Title I school and program reforms (Millsap et al., 1992; U.S. Department of Education, 1999) are not required to perform these tasks. Indeed, state and local education agencies and schools do play important roles in supporting implementation and in shaping the reforms to mesh with local circumstances (Datnow & Stringfield, 2000), but externally developed reform models, by definition, leave the specialized and time-consuming development work to others.

CRESPAR researchers have played active roles in developing and evaluating whole-school reform models. The work summarized by Datnow and Stringfield (2000) has identified a number of systemic processes by which implementation of various reform models is helped or hindered. Furthermore, data from the companion study to Prospects, the Special Strategies Study, have provided evidence that Title I schools implementing externally developed reforms may produce stronger achievement gains for disadvantaged students (Stringfield et al., 1997), and for African American students (Borman, Stringfield, & Rachuba, 1998) than do conventional Title I school programs. As Borman, D'Agostino, Wong, and Hedges (1998) noted, conventional targeted Title I programs typically are sporadic, and of limited duration. Most students move into and out of the program, and the average targeted assistance program offers only about 30 minutes per day of specialized pullout instruction. Although more research is needed, early evidence suggests that externally developed, whole-school reform models hold many advantages over the limited nature of supplemental, targeted programs.

Another set of studies performed by CRESPAR researchers and their colleagues has focused on discovering effective reforms that may be promoted by developing new Title I guidelines and policies, or by facilitating stronger school- and classroom-level implementations of existing policies. These studies have relied on reanalyses of data from the recently completed Prospects study, which was conducted from 1991 to 1994. The Prospects data set includes standardized reading and math achievement scores for a nationally representative sample of as many as 40,000 students in three grade cohorts (first, third, and seventh) from over 350 baseline Title I and non-Title I schools. In addition, Prospects provides rich survey data from the students, their principals, Title I and regular classroom teachers, and parents.

The primary objective of the congressionally mandated Prospects study was to: "compare educational achievement of those children with significant participation in Chapter 1 [now Title I] programs and comparable children who did not receive Chapter 1 services" (Augustus F. Hawkins-Robert T. Stafford Elementary and Secondary School Improvement Amendments of 1988, 102 Stat.130, 199). However, an extensive reanalysis of Prospects by Borman, Hewes, and Rachuba (2000) indicated that the study did not successfully attain this objective, and, thus, has limited utility for assessing the national impact of Title I. Borman and colleagues applied a case-matching algorithm in an attempt to identify a group of non-Title I students, similar enough to the Title I group, to serve as a quasi-experimental control group. The authors performed 28 main analyses and a number of supplemental analyses attempting to match Title I and non-Title I students based on an eight variable model, and on a more parsimonious three variable model – both of which were confirmed by separate logistic regression analyses as strong predictors of the dichotomous Title I participation/non-participation outcome. Despite these efforts, analyses of the matched Title I and control groups revealed large and statistically significant differences on the matching variables. Retaining the full sample of potential non-Title I control students, the authors drew repeated random samples of progressively smaller numbers of Title I students, until finally concluding that only 5% to 10% of the Title I participants had statistically similar controls. Although these data clearly fall short of providing national estimates of the recent effectiveness of Title I, the Prospects data set does have great utility for measuring students' longitudinal achievement growth and the numerous individual, family, classroom, and school correlates of longitudinal change. Most importantly for this discussion, Prospects permits large-scale investigations of the recent status of Title I schools, and of the characteristics of relatively successful Title I schools.

Analyses of Prospects have assessed the potential impacts on student achievement, and other important outcomes, of three of the five central principles of recent Title I legislative attempts to improve the program. By modeling the existing variability in how well or how poorly schools implement the key provisions of recent legislation, this work provides research-based evidence of the potential strength of these policy levers for improving Title I schools. Specifically, Borman, Wong, Hedges, and D'Agostino (in press) and D'Agostino, Borman, Hedges, and Wong (1998) investigated the achievement effects associated with greater coordination between Title I and local policies at, respectively, the level of the classroom and the school. This work helps address whether greater alignment and coherence of educational elements, which is perhaps the most important emphasis of the 1994 Title I legislation, is a strong policy lever for promoting improved student achievement. Second, in response to the focus of the 1994 reauthorization on strengthening teaching in high-poverty schools, Borman and Rachuba (in press) looked at differences in teacher preparation and professional development across schools of varying poverty levels, and at how these differences may impact teachers' sense of efficacy in the classroom and their use of reformed instructional practices. Finally, evaluating the call for stronger links among schools, parents, and communities, D'Agostino, Hedges, Wong, and Borman (in press) assessed the components of Title I parent-involvement initiatives that may lead to more productive home-school partnerships and to improved student achievement. I discuss this recent research in relation to each of these three principles below.

Long-standing legal provisions and implementation mechanisms designed to target the delivery of supplementary Title I services to students placed at risk have continued to stress the structural separation of categorical services from local policy and practice (Millsap et al., 1992; Orland, 1994). For instance, Borman et al. (in press) found that most Title I teachers planned and conducted their work in isolation from other school staff. In addition, the authors concluded that most Title I programs emphasized remedial instruction using materials and curricula that were different from those used in the regular classroom. Furthermore, most Title I programs pulled out targeted students from their regular classrooms, causing the students to miss valuable time to learn the core curriculum with which they were having trouble. In contrast to these categorical distinctions, Borman and colleagues found that Title I and regular classrooms that were characterized by greater curricular coherence and consistency were associated with improved reading achievement for Title I students and for the students' regular classroom peers. In addition, D'Agostino et al. (1998) found some evidence suggesting that global, school-wide coordination of Title I and local curricular and instructional policies was associated with improved math and reading achievement. Other analyses by Borman et al. (in press) suggested that Title I and regular teachers who more actively collaborated were more likely to achieve consistency and coherence in their curricular and instructional approaches. Thus, these analyses provide empirical support for the legislative focus on alignment and coordination, and suggest that providing more opportunities for active collaboration among specialists and regular classroom teachers may be one fruitful way for Title I schools to promote greater school-wide coordination and coherence.

With regard to the quality of teaching, Borman and Rachuba (in press) found that the teacher qualifications (i.e., highest degree earned, comprehensiveness of certifications, and years of experience) did not vary significantly across schools with low, medium, and high concentrations of poverty. Although many researchers have asserted that teachers in high-poverty schools are less qualified, widely used measures such as these appear to be poor indicators of the differential qualifications that teachers bring to classrooms. Alternatively, when considering opportunities for teachers' ongoing professional development (i.e., supportive in-services, collaboration among staff, participation in school decision making, and a supportive work environment conducive to teacher experimentation and learning), Borman and Rachuba found statistically significant differences favoring teachers from lower poverty schools. Teachers from schools with the highest poverty concentrations were placed at a disadvantage, relative to their peers from lower poverty schools, on all four measures of professional development opportunities. These inequalities may have stronger implications than potential inequalities in the distribution of teacher qualifications, as Borman and Rachuba's results suggested that differences in access to ongoing professional development opportunities were linked to differences in teachers' sense of efficacy and to differences in teachers' implementation of reformed instructional practices. These findings were consistent across all schools, regardless of their poverty concentrations. These empirical results support the emphasis placed by recent legislation on ongoing professional development activities for teachers in the highest poverty Title I schools. Moreover, clear linkages between this legislation and the legislative goals of alignment and coordination are suggested by the relationship between strong professional development opportunities and reformed instruction. This relationship indicates that the complex task of implementing coordinated and challenging curricula and instruction for all students may be fostered through greater investments in advancing the professional status and capacities of teachers in high-poverty schools.

The study by D'Agostino et al. (in press) examined the interrelationships among various Title I school initiatives to involve parents, different forms of parent involvement, and students' end-of-year reading achievement levels after controlling for fall reading achievement (a pretest), parental socioeconomic status, and school poverty level. The authors detected a direct relationship between Title I students' reading achievements and their parents' level of home-based learning involvement. The authors did not detect relationships between students' achievements and parents' school-based involvement activities, such as volunteering in classrooms or serving on governance committees, or between students' achievements and Title I schools' initiatives to involve parents. Parents, though, were more likely to report higher levels of home-based involvement when schools developed comprehensive programs centered on: (a) offering learning materials for families to take home; and (b) fostering school-family relations by openly communicating with parents and by engaging them in school-parent learning compacts and other agreements. Thus, the results revealed that Title I schools may indirectly influence students' reading achievement by encouraging parents to become more effective home educators. The authors concluded that in order to create parent programs promoting Title I student achievement, schools must implement a comprehensive set of procedures that get parents involved in supporting their children's learning at home.

Taken together, the results of this recent work are generally supportive of the current direction of Title I policy. Although the implementation of externally developed programs may hasten the process of reform and improvement, the history of Title I, and of education in general, suggests that change is slow. Staff from state and local education agencies must change their roles from fiscal and procedural monitors to facilitators of best practices. Title I teachers must move away from teaching disjointed, remedial classes to enabling all students to attain high performance standards. Title I schools must provide ongoing professional development opportunities and a supportive work environment to enhance the professional capacities of all teachers. To improve the total learning opportunities of Title I students, schools must work with parents in creating strong educational environments in the classroom and within the home. Title I policies appear to be focusing on principles that can make a difference, but it is also clear that far too few Title I schools are reliably responding to the new principles encouraged by recent legislation.

Conclusion

Title I has come a long way, but it has not reached its full potential. Intergovernmental conflict, poor implementation, and a lack of an achievement effect marked the first stage of the program. A second stage, during the 1970s and 1980s, was characterized by the development of increasingly specific implementation and accountability standards, federal and local cooperation, improved implementation, and growing, but modest, program effects. During the late 1980s and during the 1990s, new legislation stressed reform and improvement but, aside from some tinkering around the edges, the administration and operation of Title I remained fairly stable, and program effects remained essentially unchanged. As we begin the twenty-first century, a new stage of the program's evolution has emerged; one in which widespread implementation of research-proven programs and practices is increasingly regarded as the key to improving the effectiveness of Title I.

Recent changes to Title I offer great promise for upgrading the educational opportunities and outcomes of the nation's least-advantaged children. The 1994 law called on states to raise academic standards, to build the capacity of teachers and schools, to develop challenging new assessments, to ensure accountability by school officials, to ensure the inclusion of all children, and to develop coordinated, systemic reforms. These sweeping changes are designed to transform Title I from a supplemental remedial program to an integral component of standards-based, whole-school reform. These new policies, along with the federal government's support of research-proven, whole-school reform models, are likely to lead to improvements in the effectiveness of Title I.

However, as stated earlier, there has been uneven progress in implementing the new Title I provisions. Borman and D'Agostino (in press) noted that along with specific guidelines and stronger federal oversight to ensure implementation fidelity, it seems one of the important factors in the historical improvement of Title I was the establishment of a uniform national assessment and evaluation system – the Title I Evaluation and Reporting System (TIERS). With the transition from TIERS to the new assessments, though, consistent nationwide data on Title I students' achievements have been notably absent. Borman and D'Agostino (in press) indicated that the results from across four decades of Title I evaluation data suggest that a lack of specific guidelines and a weak, or nonexistent, accountability system should be regarded as strong warning signs. On the other hand, when states and localities are held accountable for a clear and measurable set of outputs, Title I is more likely to be implemented and it is more likely to improve student achievement. Without strong accountability mechanisms, it is likely that the implementation and effectiveness of future Title I programs will remain modest and variable.

Title I research and evaluation also have evolved considerably. The current emphasis on research-proven programs and practices is suggestive of the increasingly proactive role that research and evaluation may play in Title I program improvement. However, newly developed programs, and the vast majority of existing programs, funded by Title I require more, and better, evidence of their effects on student outcomes. As stated earlier, primarily due to the legal requirements of the program, no randomized experiments of Title I programs have ever been conducted. Perhaps facilitated by the recent Ed-Flex expansion legislation, Title I could support statewide randomized field experiments like the widely acclaimed Tennessee STAR class size study (Mosteller, Light, & Sachs, 1996; Word, et al., 1990). As currently conceived, the legislation permits all states to apply for Ed-Flex authority, allowing them to waive certain educational laws and regulations, such as those under Title I and other formula-grant programs. Although the potential is, at this time,

untapped, under the provisions of the Ed-Flex expansion legislation it may be possible to encourage states to implement new
policies involving large-scale, state-of-the-art randomized
experiments of innovative reforms (McDill & Natriello, in press).
For instance, researchers might randomly select control and
treatment sites from statewide lists of schools interested in
implementing specific externally developed reform models. Such
studies would enable researchers to collect the highest-quality data
possible on the effects of externally developed whole-school
reforms, or of other innovative reforms, and to advance Title I
research in unprecedented ways. This method of encouraging
experimentation and evaluation under the new Ed-Flex expansion
law might well provide a more proactive approach (relative to the
"trickle-down" approach implied by the systemic reform perspective of current accountability mandates) towards leveraging
evaluation to reform high-poverty Title I schools (McDill &
Natriello, in press). Through efforts such as these, research can
play an increasingly active role in the continuing evolution and
improvement of Title I.

Notes

1. In addition to the role of the summer effect, researchers have
cited other phenomena that may contribute to differing outcomes
on locally administered fall-to-spring and annual tests. For
instance, Linn, Dunbar, Harnisch, and Hastings (1982) noted that
some teachers and administrators may vary pretest and posttest
conditions in subtle ways in hopes of inflating the gains posted by
the students in their programs. When local evaluations are based
on an annual cycle, though, they typically employ the posttest as
the pretest for the following school year. Therefore, relative to
fall-to-spring cycles, annual testing cycles may provide fewer
incentives for administrators and teachers to alter testing schedules
and conditions. Slavin (1989) provides especially interesting data
from Oklahoma City Title I evaluations illustrating the differences
in effect estimates based on fall-to-spring, annual, and quasi-
experimental control group conditions.
2. As additional suggestive evidence of Title I effects, and of this
historical trend of effects, the results from the National Assessment of Educational Progress (NAEP) indicate that the achievement gaps between both African American and White students and

economically disadvantaged and advantaged students diminished during the 1970s and early 1980s (Smith & O'Day, 1991). However, from the late 1980s through the 1990s, these gaps either widened or remained unchanged (Grissmer, Kirby, Berends, & Williamson, 1994).

3. For additional information, refer to publications by the Northwest Regional Educational Laboratory (1998) and by Herman, et al. (1998), who recently cataloged and reviewed many of the more widely implemented whole-school reform models.

Author Note

The preparation of this chapter was made possible by grants from the Department of Education, Office of Educational research and Improvement (Grant No. OERI-R-117-D40005) and from the Spencer Foundation (Grant No. 199900212). The data presented, the statements made, and the views expressed are solely the responsibility of the author. Copyright 2000 by Lawrence Erlbaum Associates. Adapted by permission of the publisher. Please direct all correspondences concerning this chapter to Geoffrey D. Borman, Johns Hopkins University, 3003 North Charles Street, Suite 200, Baltimore, MD 21218. Electronic mail may be sent to gborman@csos.jhu.edu.

References

Augustus F. Hawkins-Robert T. Stafford Elemcatary and Secondary School Improvement Amendments of 1988, Pub. L. No. 100-297, 102 Stat.130 (1988).

Berman, P., & McLaughlin, M.W. (1977). *Federal programs supporting educational change. Vol.VIII, implementing and sustaining innovations.* Santa Monica, CA: RAND.

Berman, P., & McLaughlin, M.W. (1979). *Federal programs supporting educational change. Vol. VII, factors affecting implementation and continuation.* Santa Monica, CA: RAND.

Borman, G.D., & D'Agostino, J.V. (1996). Title I and student achievement: A meta-analysis of federal evaluation results. *Educational Evaluation and Policy Analysis, 4,* 309-326.

Borman, G.D., & D'Agostino, J.V. (in press). Title I and student achievement: A quantitative synthesis. In G.D. Borman, S. Stringfield, & R.E. Slavin (Eds.), *Title I: Compensatory education at the crossroads.* Mahwah, NJ: Lawrence Erlbaum Associates.

Borman, G.D., D'Agostino, J.V., Wong, K.K., & Hedges, L.V. (1998). The longitudinal achievement of Chapter 1 students: Preliminary evidence from the Prospects study. *Journal of Education for Students Placed At Risk, 3,* 363-399.

Borman, G.D., Hewes, G., & Rachuba, L.T. (2000). The impact of federal compensatory education funding: Does the congressionally mandated Prospects study inform the debate? Manuscript submitted for publication.

Borman, G.D., & Rachuba, L.T. (in press). Qualifications and professional growth opportunities of teachers in high- and low-poverty elementary schools. *Journal of Negro Education.*

Borman, G.D., Stringfield, S., & Slavin, R.E. (Eds.) (in press). *Title I: Compensatory education at the crossroads.* Mahwah, NJ: Lawrence Erlbaum Associates.

Borman, G.D., Stringfield, S., and Rachuba, L. (1998). *Advancing minority high achievement: National trends and promising programs and practices.* New York: The College Board. (ERIC Document Reproduction Service No. ED 438 380).

Borman, G.D., Wong, K.K., Hedges, L.V., & D'Agostino, J.V. (in press). Coordinating categorical and regular programs: Effects on Title I students' educational opportunities and outcomes. In G.D. Borman, S. Stringfield, & R.E. Slavin (Eds.), *Title I: Compensatory education at the crossroads.* Mahwah, NJ: Lawrence Erlbaum Associates.

Citizens' Commission on Civil Rights (1998). *Title I in midstream: The fight to improve schools for poor kids. Executive summary.* Washington, DC: Author.

Cohen, D.K. (1982). Policy and organization: The impact of state and federal education policy on school governance. *Harvard Educational Review, 52,* 474-499.

Cooper, H., Nye, B., Charlton, K., Lindsay, J., & Greathouse, S. (1996). The effects of summer vacation on achievement test scores: A narrative and meta-analytic review. *Review of Educational Research, 66,* 227-268.

Council of the Great City Schools (1999, March). *Reform and results: An analysis of Title I in the great city schools 1994-95 to 1997-98.* Washington, DC: Author.

Crandall, D. P., Loucks-Horsley, S., Baucher, J.E., Schmidt, W.B., Eiseman, J.W., Cox, P. L., Miles, M. B., Huberman, A. M.,

Taylor, B. L., Goldberg, J. A., Shive, G., Thompson, C. L., & Taylor, J.A. (1982). *Peoples, policies, and practices: Examining the chain of school improvement (vols. 1-10).* Andover, MA: The NETWORK.

Datnow, A., & Stringfield, S. (2000). Working together for reliable school reform. *Journal of Education for Students Placed At Risk, 5,* 183-204.

D'Agostino, J.V., Borman, G.D., Hedges, L.V., & Wong, K.K. (1998). Longitudinal achievement and Chapter 1 coordination in high-poverty schools: A multilevel analysis of the Prospects data. *Journal of Education for Students Placed At Risk, 3,* 401-420.

D'Agostino, J.V., Hedges, L.V., Wong, K.K., & Borman, G.D. (in press). Title I home-school partnerships: Effects on parenting practices and on student achievement. In G.D. Borman, S. Stringfield, & R.E. Slavin (Eds.), *Title I: Compensatory education at the crossroads.* Mahwah, NJ: Lawrence Erlbaum Associates.

Elementary and Secondary Education Act of 1965, Pub. L. No. 89-10, 79 Stat. 27 (1965).

Grissmer, D.W., Kirby, S.N., Berends, M., & Williamson, S. (1994). *Student achievement and the changing American family.* Santa Monica, CA: RAND.

Heyns, B. (1978). *Summer learning and the effects of schooling.* New York: Academic Press.

Herman, R., Aladjem, D., McMahon, P., Masem, E., Mulligan, I., O'Malley, A.S., Quinones, S., Reeve, A., & Woodruff, D. (1998). *An educators' guide to schoolwide reform.* Arlington, VA: Educational Research Service.

Herrington, C.D., & Orland, M.E. (1992). Politics and federal aid to urban school systems: The case of Chapter 1. In J. Cibulka, R. Reed, and K. Wong (Eds.), *The politics of urban education in the United States* (pp. 167-179). Washington, DC: Falmer Press.

Jeffrey, J.R. (1978). *Education for children of the poor: A study of the origins and implementation of the Elementary and Secondary Education Act of 1965.* Columbus, OH: Ohio State University Press.

Kennedy, M.M., Birman, B.F., & Demaline, R.E. (1986). *The effectiveness of Chapter 1 services. Second interim report from the national assessment of Chapter 1.* Washington, DC: U.S.

Department of Education, Office of Educational Research and Improvement.

Kirst, M., & Jung, R. (1982). The utility of a longitudinal approach in assessing implementation: A thirteen-year review of Title I, ESEA. In W. Williams, R.F. Elmore, J.S. Hall, R. Jung, M. Kirst, S.A. MacManus, B.J. Narver, R.P. Nathan, & R.K. Yin (Eds.), *Studying implementation* (pp. 119-148). Chatham, NJ: Chatham House.

Linn, R.L., Dunbar, S.B., Harnisch, D.L., & Hastings, C.N. (1982). The validity of the Title I evaluation and reporting system. In E. House, S. Mathison, J. Pearsol, & H. Preskill (Eds.). *Evaluation studies review annual.* (pp. 427-442). Beverly Hills, CA: Sage Publications.

Martin, R., & McClure, P. (1969). *Title I of ESEA: Is it helping poor children?* Washington, DC: Washington Research Project and NAACP Legal Defense and Educational Fund, Inc.

McDill, E., & Natriello, G. (in press). History and promise of assessment and accountability in Title I. In G.D. Borman, S. Stringfield, & R.E. Slavin (Eds.), *Title I: Compensatory education at the crossroads.* Mahwah, NJ: Lawrence Erlbaum Associates.

McLaughlin, D.H. (1977). *Title I, 1965-1975: Synthesis of the findings of federal studies.* Palo Alto, CA: American Institutes for Research.

McLaughlin, M.W. (1976). Implementation of ESEA Title I: A problem of compliance. *Teachers College Record, 77,* 397-415.

Meyer, J.W., Scott, W.R., & Strang, D. (1986). Centralization, fragmentation, and school district complexity. *Administrative Science Quarterly, 32,* 186-201.

Millsap, M.A., Turnbull, B.J., Moss, M., Brigham, N., Gamse, B., & Marks, E. (1992). *The Chapter 1 implementation study, interim report.* Cambridge, MA: Abt Associates.

Mosteller, F., Light, R.J., & Sachs, J.A. (1996). Sustained inquiry in education: Lessons from skill grouping and class size. *Harvard Educational Review, 66,* 797-842.

Northwest Regional Educational Laboratory (1998). Catalog of school reform models (1st ed.). Portland, OR: Author.

Orland, M.E. (1994). From the picket fence to the chain link fence: National goals and federal aid to the disadvantaged. In K. Wong & M. Wang (Eds.), *Rethinking policy for at-risk students* (pp. 179-196). Berkeley, CA: McCutchan.

Peterson, P.E. (1981). *City limits.* Chicago: University of Chicago Press.

Peterson, P.E., Rabe, B.G., & Wong, K.W. (1986). *When federalism works.* Washington, DC: Brookings Institution.

Rossi, R.J., McLaughlin, D.H., Campbell, E.A., & Everett, B.E. (1977). *Summaries of major Title I evaluations, 1966-1976.* Palo Alto, CA: American Institutes for Research.

Slavin, R.E. (1989). Students at risk of school failure: The problem and its dimensions. In R.E. Slavin, N.L Karweit, & N.A. Madden (Eds.), *Effective programs for students at risk* (pp. 1-19). Boston: Allyn and Bacon.

Smith, M.S. & O'Day, J.A. (1991). Educational equality: 1966 and now. In D. Verstegen & J. Ward (Eds.), *Spheres of justice in education: The 1990 American Education Finance Association yearbook* (pp. 53-100). New York: Harper Business.

Stringfield, S., Millsap, M.A., Herman, R., Yoder, N., Brigham, N., Nesselrodt, P., Schaffer, E., Karweit, N., Levin, M., & Stevens, R. (with Gamse, B., Puma, M., Rosenblum, S., Beaumont, J., Randall, B., & Smith, L.) (1997). *Urban and suburban/rural special strategies for educating disadvantaged children. Final report.* Washington, DC: U.S. Department of Education.

Tallmadge, G.K. and Wood, C.T. (1981). *User's guide to the ESEA Title I evaluation and reporting system.* Mountain View, CA: RMC Research Corporation.

Timpane, M. (1976). Evaluating Title I again? In C. Abt (Ed.), *The evaluation of social programs* (pp. 415-423). Beverly Hills, CA: Sage.

U.S. Department of Education (1999). *Promising results, continuing challenges: The final report of the national assessment of Title I. Executive summary.* (Prepublication copy). Washington, DC: Author.

Wargo, M. J., Tallmadge, G. K., Michaels, D. D. Lipe, D., & Morris, S. J. (1972). ESEA Title I: A reanalysis and synthesis of evaluation data from fiscal year 1965 through 1970. Palo Alto, CA: American Institutes for Research.

Word, E., Johnston, J., Bain, H.P., Fulton, B.D., Zaharias, J.B., Achilles, C.M., Lintz, M.N., Folger, J., & Breda, C. (1990). *Student/Teacher Achievement Ratio (STAR): Tennessee's K-3 class size study: Final summary report, 1985-1990.* Nashville: Tennessee State Department of Education.

CHAPTER 3

TITLE I PULLOUT PROGRAMS: BOON OR BOONDOGGLE?

Pamela S. Angelle

Introduction

The Title I program reaches ninety percent of all school districts in the country and nearly twenty percent of all elementary school students (Jakubowski & Ogletree, 1993). Title I accounted for as much as twenty percent of the total budget for the US Department of Education in the nineteen eighties (Birman, 1988), and by 1997, the program received a federal allocation of $7 billion (Puma, Karweit, Price, Ricciuti, Thompson, & Vaden-Kiernan, 1997), with a promise of continued growth into the next century (Stringfield, 1991).

During the initial years of the Title I program, misunderstandings and lack of experience with federal funding for public school education led to funds being used for general aid to schools (Martin & McClure, 1969), rather than for improving the quality of education for indigent students. For example, some Georgia districts made Title I projects available to all schools. In Louisiana, approximately one third of the districts "loaned" equipment to schools that were ineligible for Title I funding. The loaned equipment, however, was often "set in concrete or fastened to the plumbing" (Martin & McClure, 1969, p.9), making its return dubious.

Discovery of these and other misuses of funds led Congress to mandate that Title I monies supplement state and local funding, but not supplant that funding. Failure to use Title I monies for supplemental services could, and occasionally did, lead to federal action to recover the misspent funds. As a means of following the letter of the law, districts across the country adopted a policy of removing students targeted for Title I services from the regular classroom. This model of providing services became known as "pullout." An examination of the effects of the pullout model is the focus of this chapter.

Support, Criticism, and Research on Pullout Programs

The typical pullout program removes targeted students from their regular class for twenty to forty minute periods to work in an individual, or more commonly, a small group setting usually on skills for reading or mathematics, or both. Although use of pullout programs is widespread - Anstrom (1995) reported that during the 1991-1992 school year, 74% of elementary schools offered some form of pullout - a search of the literature reveals scant research about these programs. Studies that exist point to positive outcomes less often than to negative outcomes, as described below.

Support for Pullout Programs
Recurrent in the literature on the pullout model are four points offered in support of the model. The first point is that it is more efficient to provide individualized activities in a one-on-one or small group setting than in a regular classroom. Rossi and DuBois (1995) found that tutorial activities are most beneficial when the instructional group is limited in size; for example, ten or fewer students. Such small numbers are common in Title I pullout classes. Special instructional activities and one-on-one teaching cannot be efficiently managed in a classroom where the majority of students do not utilize, or benefit from, the instruction being offered, according to Rossi and DuBois.

A second point in favor of the pullout model is that individualized and small group instruction provides the student with greater teacher attention than would be available in a regular classroom, where the population averages 27 or more students (Glass & Smith, 1977). Indeed, gains have been reported in Title

I programs for students in early elementary schooling and in mathematics programs (Birman, 1988). Similar gains, however, were not found in later years of schooling, nor were reading gains as great as those in mathematics (Birman, 1988; Borman, this book).

Third, proponents posit that removing students with special needs from the classroom allows the regular teacher to continue with more challenging assignments for the students who remain (Rossi & DuBois, 1995). This can be done without overwhelming the students who are pulled out precisely because they struggle with basic assignments.

Finally, those who support the pullout model argue that it reduces the chance of students being ridiculed. In contrast to opponents of pullout who argue that removing students from class stigmatizes them, proponents counter that students who remain in class to receive special instruction are at least equally stigmatized. Special services that are provided in the regular classroom call attention to the alternative instruction and less advanced content used with the children (Rossi & DuBois, 1995). These teaching strategies and the lesson content are hidden from the other students when the pullout model is used.

Criticisms of Pullout Programs

In response to each of the above supporting points, critics question whether "additional" instruction is being received in the pullout classes. Given that students who are pulled out miss instruction in the regular class, often reading and language arts instruction (Anstrom, 1995), while receiving Title I services, the pullout model seems to violate the federal requirement that Title I services supplement, not supplant, already available educational services (Jakubowski & Ogletree, 1993).

In addition, the benefits of small group instruction are greater when the instruction is sustained over a period of time. However, students who receive instruction in Title I small groups do so in small doses, usually only once or twice a week and then for relatively short periods of time. Moreover, any gains made are lost when students discontinue the Title I services (Birman, 1988). Thus, rather than remediate learning deficits, critics (Anderson & Pellicer, 1990) assert that pullout results in fragmentation of the curriculum for struggling students. Consequently, an unintended outcome of pullout programs has been that students become "lifers" (Anderson & Pellicer, 1990, p.11), rather than gaining skills and exiting the program.

Such an outcome raises issues regarding program purpose. As noted, the historical impetus for pullout programs stemmed from mandates to satisfy federal regulations regarding expenditures of Title I funds. Timar (1994) noted that this strategy begs the question of priority. Is the primary goal, he asks, to assure expenditure of funds on only those students meeting eligibility criteria, or is the purpose to provide quality instruction for low-income, low-achieving students? As long as compliance is the byword, schools that fail to teach students, but spend the monies as mandated, escape sanction. Thus, the children themselves, not the quality of their education, become the program target (Glass & Smith, 1977; Timar, 1994), with lackluster results for the children.

While conceding that some regulation is necessary to ensure that federal funds are used for the benefit of students, Timar (1994) asserts that the result of the strict compliance monitoring is that professional judgment has been undercut and authority fragmented. Arguing that "funding should target schools, not students" (p.61), Timar maintains that the focus should be on the richness of the learning experience, the organization of the curricula, and the needs of the students.

Research on Pullout Programs

There is a dearth of research on pullout programs, as noted earlier. As a result, studies not only of Title I pullout programs, but of other pullout programs as well are reported here.

The research reveals overlapping problems with the pullout model. These problems include (a) missed instruction in the regular classroom (Rossi & DuBois, 1995; Glass & Smith, 1977; Anstrom, 1995) (b) lack of curricular integration (Bean, Colley, Eichelberger, Lazar, & Zigmond, 1991; Birman, 1988), (c) lack of communication between teachers (Birman, 1988; Anderson & Pellicer, 1990; Glass & Smith, 1977; Rossi & DuBois, 1995), (d) quality of instruction in the pullout setting (Anderson & Pellicer, 1990; Glass & Smith, 1977; Birman, 1988) and (e) stigmatizing effects of pullout participation (Rossi & DuBois, 1995; Glass & Smith, 1977). Each of these concerns is addressed below.

Missed Instruction in the Regular Classroom. A problem that impairs the effectiveness of pullout programs is that students, who already lag behind their classmates academically, are placed at further disadvantage by missing instruction in the regular class while they are removed to work with the Title I specialist. This impact was clearly demonstrated by Rossi and DuBois (1995), who found that regular teachers saw little connection between content taught in the regular class and that taught by the Title I teacher. The negative effects of missing regular class instruction affected students across levels. High school students who were pulled for Title I instruction were prevented from earning graduation credit while they were in the tutorial setting (Rossi & DuBois, 1995). Moreover, Anstrom (1995) notes that the time taken away from the regular instruction normally is taken away from the core subjects of math and reading, classes which the student who has academic difficulty can ill afford to miss.

In the Rossi and DuBois (1995) study, regular teachers also expressed concern that children who were pulled out fell further behind because of the time spent away from class. This finding corroborates earlier work by Glass and Smith (1977), who reported a consistently negative relationship between the percentage of time that pupils were in the pullout class and their achievement in math and reading. Such findings suggest that disadvantaged students who are struggling to keep up are in fact further compromised in their learning efforts, with the result that they fail to move toward the same achievement levels of students not in pullout programs.

Lack of Curricular Integration. Compounding the problem of missing instruction in the regular class is the lack of integration between content taught in the regular and pullout settings. A study by Bean, Cooley, Eichelberger, Lazar, and Zigmond (1991) compared pullout instruction with in-class instruction in a remedial reading program. These researchers found that both the materials and targeted skills in the two settings were unrelated. Specialists in the pullout program often used supplemental materials, rather than materials used in the regular program. Even though the specialists attempted to fit in with the regular class procedures, instructional strategies and materials used in the regular classroom were difficult to transfer to the remedial setting.

Likewise, Birman (1988) cited research (Allington, 1986) that found poor coordination between the regular teacher and the Title I teacher, a weakness that resulted in difficulties for the pulled out student. Disadvantaged students who enter the Title I program with academic weaknesses find themselves struggling to connect content taught in the Title I class with that taught in the regular classroom. This problem can often be credited to the lack of time available for collegial planning which would allow the regular and Title I teachers to coordinate curricular content.

Lack of Communication Between Teachers.   Given that little cohesion exists between the content taught by the regular and pullout teachers, there is no surprise that researchers find concurrently that little communication occurs between the teachers (Birman, 1988; Rossi & DuBois, 1995). When these teachers do communicate, Birman reported that it is often a cursory exchange about a student, rather than a jointly planned lesson. Thus, the students are forced to adjust to the varied teaching styles and curricular content of the regular and pullout programs with little or no assistance from the teachers.

Part of the problem for this lack of communication may rest with the district. School administrators who receive a mandate to implement the pullout may not understand the best way to integrate this model into the school's curriculum. An unclear view of the Title I program on the part of the principal can have a rippling effect throughout the school, leading to communication problems at several levels (Anderson & Pellicer, 1990).

In this context, the matter of who is responsible for the education of students in pullout programs becomes problematic. Regular teachers tend to feel that their responsibility is diminished in proportion to the amount of time the child is with the specialist, particularly because the time spent in pullout is intended to build the basic skills of the child (Rossi & DuBois, 1995; Glass & Smith, 1977). On the other hand, the specialist often feels that her/his prescribed responsibility is constrained to remedial instruction, and that the regular teacher has primary responsibility for student learning.

Quality of Instruction in the Pullout Setting.   The quality of instruction available to students in pullout programs is sometimes questionable. In some cases, pullout services are provided by an aide or tutor. The strategy of hiring less expensive aides and tutors brings substantial cost savings to the district, but the cost effectiveness is questionable. As Birman (1988) notes, using aides in lieu of certified teachers contributes to the low quality of the overall education of Title I students.

More typically, teacher specialists provide the instruction for students in pullout programs. Though these specialists are certified teachers, they are often only slightly better trained than regular teachers (Glass & Smith, 1977), and receive fewer than ten hours per academic year in additional staff development. Thus, the problem of limited time in the small group setting, discussed earlier, is compounded by the inadequate training of the teacher specialist.

Teachers in compensatory programs also face the choice of teaching students at their current level, or preparing them for state mandated testing. Anderson and Pellicer (1990) report students end up doing remedial work, which often consists of little more than completing worksheets. As a consequence, Title I students score poorly on state tests. This kind of unimaginative teaching lends credence to the assertion of Anderson and Pellicer that the selection of the Title I staff is as important as the delivery model in determining the effectiveness of the program.

The quality of instruction in some Title I programs is further diminished when pullout services are provided by an aide or a tutor, rather than a certified teacher. Though the strategy of hiring less expensive aides brings substantial cost savings to the district, cost effectiveness is questionable. Using aides in lieu of certified teachers contributes to low quality in the overall education of Title I students (Birman, 1988).

Stigmatizing Effects of Pullout Participation. Those for and against pullout programs have long debated the stigma of being labeled a "special" student. The adverse effects on the student's self esteem and the feeling of inferiority in the eyes of peers are concerns. However, the most controversial aspect of labeling comes from the teachers' behavior toward those students who are pulled out for special instruction (Glass & Smith, 1977; Rossi & DuBois, 1995).

Title I teachers and aides often have low expectations of their students, and, as a result, treat them differently, as a study by Glass and Smith (1977) found. Title I students were regarded by their teachers as "intellectually slow" or "academically weak" and achieved academically by as much as one-quarter standard deviation below that of students who were comparably weak but not labeled. Moreover, attention to and support for these labeled students were reduced by one-third standard deviation below those not labeled. Glass and Smith (1977) describe these findings were "most pertinent and startling" (p.5), and conclude that while labeling a student as "slow" or "dull" has a modest effect on academic achievement, it has a substantial effect on the teacher's judgment of the student's potential success.

Schoolwide Programs as an Alternative to Pullout

As funding increases and the number of students who are served by Title I throughout the United States likewise increases, the question that educators and policy makers must ask is how can the children best be served? Are schoolwide programs or pull out programs the optimum model? While pullout continues to be the most common intervention used in Title I programming (Anstrom, 1995; Saint-Laurent, 1996), concerns enumerated above remain regarding its use.

As early as the nineteen-seventies, Glass and Smith (1977) proposed that *all* pupils in low-SES schools deserve countervailing funding. Specifically, they argued that large concentrations of low-achieving students have indirect, negative effects on those students at the school who are above average in achievement.

The Hawkins-Stafford Amendments of 1988, as well as the 1994 Improving America's School Act, allowed schools to receive funding to implement Title I programs schoolwide. Schoolwide programs allow for greater flexibility in the use of funding to meet the needs of all students in the school (Wong & Meyer, 1998). Key components addressed through schoolwide programs include an emphasis on prevention (New York City Board of Education, 1990), parental involvement and education (reported as strengthened in over three-fourths of the programs), and more inclusive staff development (reported teacher training included more total hours than in traditional Title I schools). These components enable districts to focus on phasing out pullout programs and integrating the Title I curriculum with that of the rest of the school, thereby improving the effectiveness of the entire school rather than "targeting" those identified as disadvantaged.

Moreover, integration of Title I services removes the fragmentation of the program as a result of categorical stipulations (Wong & Meyer, 1998).

Wong and Meyer (1998) note that schoolwide programs allow schools to help students when the need arises, rather than delaying services until a designated time, as occurs through the more rigid pullout model. Moreover, these schoolwide programs foster greater coordination between the regular instruction program and the Title I program (Wong & Meyer, 1998). According to a study of schoolwide programs by Taylor and Teddlie (1997), when students were pulled out of the regular class, teachers report that the pullout activities were coordinated with the Title I teacher. Similarly, Bean, et al. (1991) found that with the schoolwide model, students frequently worked with the specialist in a tutoring mode in the in-class setting. Thus, students remained in class with the other students but they and their classmates had access to the assistance of the specialist.

The U.S. Department of Education (1993) surveyed principals throughout the United States who utilized schoolwide programs and found that eighty-five percent reported positive results from their projects. The principals noted the increased flexibility in service delivery, the offer of assistance to all students, rather than a targeted few, and the elimination of the negative aspects of pullout.

Another potential benefit of the schoolwide option is improved accountability. Title I programs must now include state content and performance standards that are set for all students. Aligning Title I programs to the state standards and assessments increases the likelihood that instructional practices in Title I classes will meet the same accountability expectations of regular classes (Wong & Meyer, 1998).

The schoolwide model is not without critics, however. Some schools view schoolwide programs as risky. The school is still mandated to demonstrate academic gains under the short evaluation cycle of Title I. Because schoolwide programs are more complex than the small group pullout programs, success is uncertain (Burnett, 1993). Schools that change to schoolwide programs must be prepared to provide staff development in new standards-based content and effective teaching will be necessary, as well as communication with parents and community as the transition is made (Anstrom, 1995).

Recommendations from the Field

Recommendations for policy found in the literature generally fall along two lines. First, the focus of program effort should be on *schools* instead of *children*. Funding should be based on the number of disadvantaged children in the school, not the number qualifying for Title I assistance (Timar, 1994; Glass & Smith, 1977). As an instrument for changing schools, effective Title I programs should be invisible, that is, indistinguishable from the services for all children (Timar, 1994; Wong & Meyer, 1998).

Second, the focus should shift from implementing remedial programs for specific student needs to creating effective learning environments for all students (Timar, 1994; Birman, 1988; Wong & Meyer, 1998). High expectations for all students strengthen the overall school organization. Continued research is warranted to identify organizational changes needed to serve all students in all schools.

Summary and Conclusion

Removing students from the regular classroom for specialized instruction is a common practice in school systems throughout the United States. In this smaller setting students can receive more individualized instruction and greater teacher attention. However, the benefits come at a price. Students pulled out of the regular classroom may be forced to correlate the special instruction with the regular class instruction on their own. In addition, the stigmatizing effect of being pulled out of the classroom for extra instruction often results in the student being labeled as special for the duration of the student's educational career.

The educational concepts of compliance and supplanting are far removed from the needs of disadvantaged children. A return to the concepts for which Title I funding was established in the first place is needed. If the goal is the education of disadvantaged children, then these children must be challenged to reach higher levels of achievement.

Title I programs that are implemented schoolwide can be beneficial to disadvantaged students through the flexibility offered by this model. However, principals and teachers alike should be aware of the academic challenges faced by these students. Professional collaboration with teacher specialists, teacher modeling of accepting differences, and expectations that all children can achieve, will ensure not only that federal dollars are being spent wisely but that the investment made in the future of the children is a solid investment.

References

Anderson, L.W. & Pellicer, L. O. (1990). Synthesis of Research on Compensatory and Remedial Education. *Educational Leadership, 48* (1), 10-16.

Anstrom, K. (1995). New Directions for Chapter 1/Title I. *Directions-in-Language-and-Education,1* (7), 694-701.

Bean, R. M., Cooley, W. W., Eichelberger, R. T., Lazar, M.K., and Zigmond, N. (1991). Inclass or Pullout: Effects of Setting on the Remedial Reading Program. *Journal of Reading Behavior, 23* (4), 445-463.

Birman, B. F. (1988). How to Improve a Successful Program. *American Educator, 12* (1), 22-29.

Borman, G. D., & D'Agostino, J. V. (1996). Title I and student achievement: A meta-analysis of federal evaluation results. *Educational Evaluation and Policy Analysis, 4,* 309-326.

Burnett, G. (1993). *Chapter 1 Schoolwide Projects: Advantages and Limitations.* (ERIC/CUE Digest, 92). New York: ERIC Clearinghouse on Urban Education. (ERIC Document Reproduction Service No. ED 363 668)

Glass, G. V. and Smith, M. L. (1977). *Pull Out in Compensatory Education.* Colorado University: Boulder Laboratory of Educational Research. (ERIC Document Reproduction Service No. ED 160 723)

Jakubowski, D. and Ogletree, E. J. (1993). *The Effectiveness of Chapter 1 Pull-Out Programs on Reading Achievement.* (ERIC Document Reproduction Service No. ED 367 734)

Jenkins, J. R., Jewell, M., Leicester, N., O'Connor, R. E., Jenkins, L. M., & Troutner, N. (1994) Accommodations for individual differences without classroom ability groups: An experiment in school restructuring. *Exceptional Children, 60,* 344-358.

Martin, R., & McClure, P. (1969). *Title I of ESEA: Is it helping poor children?* Washington, DC: Washington Research Project.

New York City Board of Education (1990). *Beyond remediation: School Based Strategies for Reducing Education Risk. Research Brief #3.* New York: Office of Research, Evaluation, and Assessment. (ERIC Document Reproduction Service No. 325 583).

Puma, M. J., Karweit, N., Price, C., Ricciuti, A., Thompson, W., & Vaden-Kiernan, M. (1997). *Prospects: Final report on student outcomes.* Bethesda, MD: Abt Associates.

Rossi, R. J. and DuBois, P. (1995) *Evaluation of Projects Funded by the School Dropout Demonstration Assistance Program. Volume 1: Findings and Recommendations.* Palo Alto, CA: American Institutes for Research in the Behavioral Sciences. (ERIC Document Reproduction Service No. 389 063)

Saint-Laurent, Lise (1996). *PIER: An Inclusive Model for At-Risk Students.* Paper presented at the Annual International Convention of the Council for Exceptional Children, Orlando, Florida.

Stringfield, S., Billig, S. H., and Davis, A. (1991). Implementing a Research Based Model of Chapter 1 Program Improvement. *Phi Delta Kappan, 72* (8), 600-607.

Taylor, D. L. & Teddlie, C. (1999). Implementation fidelity in Title I schoolwide programs. *Journal of Education for Students Placed at Risk, 4,* 299-319.

Timar, T. (1994). Federal Education Policy and Practice: Building Organizational Capacity Through Chapter 1. *Education Evaluation and Policy Analysis, 16* (1), 51-66.

U. S. Department of Education. (1993). *Reinventing Chapter 1: The current Chapter 1 program and new directions, final report of the national assessment of the chapter program.* Washington, DC: Author.

Welch, M., Richards, G. Okada, R., Richards, J., & Prescott, S. (1995). A consultation and paraprofessional pull-in system of service delivery: A report on student outcomes and teacher satisfaction. *Remedial and Special Education, 16,* 16-28.

Wong, K. K. and Meyer, S. J. (1998). Title I Schoolwide Programs: A Synthesis of Findings From Recent Evaluation. *Educational Evaluation and Policy Analysis, 20* (2), 115-136.

SECTION II.

Title I Schoolwide Programs:
Evidence from the Field

CHAPTER 4

DIFFERENT ROADS TO SUCCESS:
A COMPARISON OF TITLE I PROGRAMS
IN ONE SOUTHERN SCHOOL DISTRICT

Dianne L. Taylor & Charles B. Teddlie

The two schools we describe in this chapter were studied as part of a multi-year evaluation study of 30 Title I schoolwide programs in a large deep South district. Information from this evaluation has been presented in a variety of publications and presentations (e.g., Taylor & Teddlie, 1998, 1999a, 1999b; Teddlie, Kochan, & Taylor, 2000).

We selected these schools because they provide an interesting contrast regarding different roads to successful schoolwide programs. Though both schools served demographically similar students, their schoolwide programs differed in many ways. These programmatic differences appear to be associated with other differences found on various attitudinal, behavioral, and cognitive (achievement) variables.

One of the schools implemented Success for All (SFA), one of the "Special Strategies" for school improvement promoted through the Comprehensive School Reform Demonstration (CSRD) model described in Chapter 9 of this volume (Meza, Dahlkemper, & Buttram). The other school implemented an improvement plan developed by a school acting on its own.

Title I programs in general have often been criticized for not generating "true" school change, and the CSRD has been put forth as a process for generating that change. Reynolds, Teddlie,

Hopkins, and Stringfield (2000) elaborated on the CSRD model, commenting about:

> the potential utility for improvement of "off the shelf" models of school improvement which do not require school invention, or elaboration. The United States shows numbers of these such as those featured in the Special Strategies evaluation of Stringfield and colleagues (Stringfield, et al., 1994, 1997), including Slavin's *Success for All* initiative, the *Coalition of Essential Schools*, the *Comer Programme* and the *Paidea Programme* .... The potential re-conceptualizing of staff development activities towards the provision of foundational material may well be likely to replace the more "do it yourself" discovery orientation that has characterized school improvement .... (p. 231)

While these Special Strategies have the potential to transform Title I schoolwide programs in a positive direction, three important caveats must be taken into consideration.

- There is convincing evidence from the school effectiveness research literature that school *context factors must be taken into consideration* when designing an improvement project. Researchers have demonstrated that the correlates of effective schooling work only under appropriate contextual conditions (e.g, Hallinger and Murphy, 1986; Teddlie and Stringfield, 1993). Special Strategies should take these local contextual factors into consideration; some (e.g., Accelerated Schools) do more so than others (e.g,, Success for All).

- Special Strategies *must impact the instructional core of the school*, consisting of both instructional practices and faculty culture, if meaningful change is to occur (Fullan, 1993). There is much evidence that such change, especially in teacher behavior in the classroom, is very difficult to attain (e.g., David, 1991; Elmore, 1995; Keller and Soler, 1994; Taylor and Teddlie, 1992, 1996).

- *Faculty capacity to plan, carry out, and sustain meaningful educational change should constitute a major component* of the staff development associated with any Special Strategy. Strategies that focus primarily on technical changes, or that rely too heavily on external change agents, are unlikely to result in meaningful, long-term school improvement.

This chapter provides some preliminary evidence regarding the success of one Special Strategy as opposed to school generated Title I schoolwide improvement plans. While the evidence is limited to two schools, some interesting themes emerge related to this important distinction in the structure of the two Title I schoolwide programs.

Methodology Employed for the Comparative Case Studies

Design and Methodology

These case studies are examples of the Yin (1994) Type IV case study design, with multiple cases (two) and embedded units (students within classes within schools). Spradley's (1979, 1980) componential analysis process was used in distinguishing differences between the two schools, resulting in an overall contrast table presented at the end of the chapter.

These two case studies employed multiple sources of data, some of which were qualitative (narrative) and some of which were quantitative (numeric); therefore, the overall methodology was mixed (Tashakkori & Teddlie, 1998). Data sources included the following:

- the Title I plan of each school, which was analyzed for goals and strategies;
- achievement scores (norm referenced tests and criterion referenced tests, or NRTs and CRTs);
- interviews conducted with principals, teachers, and other instructional staff;
- attitudinal questionnaires administered to the principal and samples of teachers and students;
- the teacher attitudinal questionnaires for each school contained open-ended items specific to the Title I school improvement plan (e.g., goals and strategies) at that particular site;
- student attitudinal questionnaires contained open-ended items specific to the assets and liabilities of the school,
- classroom observations including scripting, ratings on the Components of Effective Teaching (CET), which was the state sanctioned classroom observational system, plus a measure of time-on-task (TOT) (e.g., Stallings, 1980); and

- informal observations taken throughout the course of the site visits.

To gather our data, teams of four people visited each school for a day. While there, these researchers interviewed teachers selected using a stratified random sampling procedure to ensure that at least one teacher from each grade, kindergarten through fifth, was interviewed. The principal was also interviewed. An interview protocol was used and contained the same items for teachers and the principal. During the visit, attitudinal question-naires were distributed to the principal and to all of the teachers, and were administered to a sample of students from three ran-domly selected classes in Grades 3 - 5.

Where possible, items on the questionnaires completed by the principal, teachers, and students were worded to be parallel. Items asked about school climate, the principal's leadership, teacher involvement in school decision making, staff development, and job satisfaction. Response choices were arrayed Likert style, though anchors varied. Unless otherwise noted, our discussion of the questionnaire results combines the most positive or negative responses. For example, the percentage of students or teachers who responded "Very Important" and "Important," or "Strongly Disagree" and "Disagree," were combined. All data were collected during School Year (SY) 1998-99.

Observations occurred in at least one-fourth of the classrooms in each school using the CET and the TOT measures. Scripting was used to record classroom events. Observers then completed the CET, which is a measure of teacher effectiveness. The scoring scale on the CET ranged from 1 = "Unsatisfactory" to 4 = "Demonstrates Excellence." To measure students' time-on-task, a modification of the Stallings' (1980) Classroom Snapshot was used.

Data Collection at Middleville Elementary

At one of the schools, Middleville Elementary School (all names in this chapter are pseudonyms), 36 of the 38 teachers returned the attitudinal questionnaire. Questionnaires were also completed by 57 students. Interviews were held with the principal and eight of the teachers. Observations were conducted in nine of the 28 regular classrooms at Middleville.

Data Collection at Rivertown Elementary

At Rivertown Elementary School, the other school, the principal and 24 of the 31 teachers returned the attitudinal questionnaires. Questionnaires were also completed by 51 students. Interviews were held with the Rivertown principal, the Success For All coordinator, and seven teachers. One teacher from each grade level was interviewed. Observations were conducted in nine classrooms at Rivertown.

The following two sections of this chapter contain descriptions of the results of the case studies at each school. The narrative for each school will include a description of the general characteristics of the school, a description of the elements of the Title I plan and its implementation, information regarding teachers' classroom performance, staff development at the school, perceptions of school leadership, and impressions of school climate. The Middleville case study will be presented first followed by Rivertown.

Middleville Elementary School

General Characteristics

Middleville Elementary School was built in the late 1940s, but had a "cared for" appearance. The principal, faculty, students, and staff put considerable effort into making the campus attractive. Flower beds dotted the lawns, classrooms were freshly painted and windows curtained, and the grounds were free of trash and debris.

Approximately 570 students in pre-kindergarten through fifth grade attended Middleville in SY 1998-99. For an inner-city school, the student body was fairly stable. Of the students in the third, fourth or fifth grades who completed questionnaires, 73% indicated that they had attended Middleville for three or more years. The Middleville student body was considerably more stable than the Rivertown student body, as will be seen in that section of the chapter.

According to information contained in the Title I plan for the SY 1998-99, 83% of the children at Middleville were considered economically deprived. The school was located in an African American community and 77% of the students were described in the Title I plan as African American. Another 20% of the students were described as white, and 3% as other ethnicity. Many of the students who were not African American participated in a program for gifted students that the district had placed at the school to attract white students to this inner city location.

The stability of the faculty was a contrast to that of the students. Among the teachers who completed a questionnaire, 77% said they had been at the school for less than five years, while only 11% had been at Middleville for more than 10 years. The principal, Ms. Logan, had been at the school for three years and commented that staff turnover was a problem at the school.

The school district in which Middleville and Rivertown are located gives the Iowa Test of Basic Skills (ITBS) annually to third and fifth graders. Scores on the ITBS for the Spring 1999 were high for the student population served at Middleville, ranging within the second and third quartiles for reading, language, mathematics, and on the composite total for the test. At the third grade level, students scored at the 40th percentile in reading, at the 60th percentile in language arts, at the 52nd percentile in mathematics, and at the 44th percentile on the composite total. The fifth grade students scored at 47th percentile in reading, at the 63rd percentile in language arts, at the 54rd percentile in mathematics, and at the 53rd percentile on the composite total.

Fourth grade students at Middleville took the state administered CRT in the Spring 1999. Altogether 56% of the students scored at the basic, proficient, or advanced levels on the English/Language Arts section of this CRT, while 55% of the students scored at these levels on the mathematics section of this CRT. These scores exceeded the state average fourth grade scores, which is quite good for a school with such a high percentage of low-SES students, and indicate that students at Middleville were doing quite well, independent of the gifted program at the school.

Title I Plan and Its Implementation at Middleville

The year we studied Middleville was at least the third year the school had participated in the Title I schoolwide program. According to an analysis of the Title I plans (1996-97 to 1998-99), a total of $485,928, or almost a half of a million dollars, in Title I funds had been received by the school for this three year period (K. T. Associates, 2000).

For Fiscal Year (FY) 1998-99, 9% of the Middleville Title I budget was spent on salaries; over 80% was spent on equipment and supplies, including classroom and student kits and supplies,

TVs, VCRs, etc. This expenditure of Title I funds is quite different from that at Rivertown, as we will see.

For the remainder of this section of the chapter, we focus discussion on the instructional aspects of the Middleville Title I plan. Two Title I goals related to instruction and/or staff development were identified in our analysis of the SY 1998-99 plan: (1) building students' skills in reading and mathematics, and (2) raising teachers' expectations. These goals were to be accomplished by implementing 15 strategies, nine of which pertained to instruction, while six related to staff development. The instructional goals and strategies are presented in Table 1.

Table 1. Middleville Elementary School: Title I Instructional Goals and Related Strategies for Implementation

Goals
1.   Increase basic skills in reading and mathematics
2.   Raise teacher expectations
Instruction
1.   Mathematics specialist
2.   Team teaching with mathematics specialist
3.   Hands-on instruction
4.   Computer assisted instruction
5.   Thematic units
6.   Collaborative learning strategies
7.   Multiple intelligences
8.   Self-directed learning
9.   Higher order thinking skills
Staff Development Topics
1.   Diversity
2.   Collaborative planning
3.   Integrated language
4.   Writing across the curriculum
5.   Grade level curriculum standards
6.   Raise teacher expectations

Instructional goals and strategies. Our study examined the extent to which the school was moving toward the accomplishment of its Title I goals. Therefore, we assessed the extent to which instructional strategies named in the Title I plan were being implemented in classrooms.

Table 2 indicates the frequency with which the instructional strategies named in the Title I plan were observed in nine regular classes in which observations took place. The most frequently observed activity was the use of multiple intelligences, observed in three classes. Hands-on strategies and lessons that involved opportunities for higher order thinking were observed in two classes. An example of a lesson that incorporated these three strategies was a class in which students studied life cycles from childhood to adulthood. They concluded by drawing a picture of themselves as adults and writing brief a description of their picture.

Other instructional strategies targeted in the Title I plan were thematic teaching and cooperative learning, both of which were observed in one class. Use of computers and self-directed learning strategies were not observed. A strategy for improving students' mathematics skills, which was not included in Table 2, was hiring a math specialist who would team teach with other faculty. While we did not observe team teaching, several teachers noted in open-ended comments on the questionnaire that demonstration teaching was provided by the math specialist.

In addition to assessing the implementation of the instructional strategies named in the Title I plan, we asked observers to record the extent to which other attributes of good teaching were evident, specifically the strength of academic press, the effectiveness of classroom management, and the quality classroom climate. Because of pressure in the district to raise test scores, observers also recorded whether activities were primarily oriented toward skill building. The bottom half of Table 2 lists these attributes.

Lessons in seven of the nine classes had a distinct focus on skill building and drill, including completing worksheets and answering questions that required memory, but little thought. This emphasis is at odds with the strategy in the school's Title I plan to teach to multiple intelligences and engage students' higher order thinking.

Nonetheless, observers also noted lessons with strong academic press. Lessons were well planned and organized; transitions were rapid and smooth. In each class where academic press was strong, classroom management was also effective and the climate positive. Effective management was also observed in four classes when academic press was neutral, and climate positive in two classes, where academic press was neutral.

Table 2. Middleville Elementary School: Instructional Strategies in the Title I Plan and Number of Times Observed in Classrooms

Instructional strategy	Times observed
Use of hands-on instruction	2
Use of computer assisted instruction	0
Integrate curriculum by using thematic units	1
Use of cooperative learning strategies	1
Teach to multiple intelligences	3
Use strategies that promote self-directed learning	0
Provide opportunities for higher order thinking	2
Other Observed Attributes	
Knowledge/skill building/drill	7
Strong academic press	3
Effective classroom management	7
Positive classroom climate	5
Weak academic press	2
Ineffective classroom management	2
Negative classroom climate	2

NOTE: Observations occurred in 9 classrooms of regular students.

In classes with strong academic press, teachers created a warm, work-oriented environment, held high expectations for students, supported students' efforts, and kept students involved in the lesson. Conversely, weak academic press, ineffective class-room management, and a negative classroom climate were observed in two classes. In these classes, students either sat idly while the teacher attended to chores, such as checking students' work one at a time, or the teacher struggled unsuccessfully to curb off-task behavior.

Teachers' Classroom Performance at Middleville

Time-on-task (TOT) data were also collected during the observations. Interactive TOT (that portion of the time that teachers interacted with students) was 61%, and Total TOT (that portion of the time that students were either interacting with the teacher or attending to assignments) was 68%. This level of on-task behavior is higher than that reported by Teddlie and Stringfield (1993) as associated with more effective schools.

The data from the CET, presented in Table 3, corroborate the findings detailed above. The CET has two domains, instructional and management. The average score for Middleville on the 13 instructional indicators was 3.0. A score of "3" on any indicator reflects an "area of strength" and is evidence that teachers consistently meet and sometimes exceed standard. Teachers at Middleville scored an average of "3" or above on the following seven indicators: accurately presenting subject matter (3.7); presenting content at developmentally appropriate levels (3.5); communicating effectively with students (3.4); sequencing lessons to promote learning (3.3); using available materials to achieve lesson objectives (3.1); encouraging students' participation (3.1); and developing the lesson effectively (3.0).

The lowest score for Middleville teachers was for relating relevant examples or events to content, for which the score was 2.5, the mid-point of the scale. A score of 2 indicates an "area of need," which indicates that although performance meets expectations sometimes, staff development activities are needed. The average score for the management indicators at Middleville was 3.1. Teachers scored at or above 3.0 on all six indicators, indicating that teachers' management skills were strong.

In summary, despite problems with teacher turnover, most Middleville teachers had strong instructional and classroom management skills, and maintained on-task behavior in their classes. Perhaps a by-product of the strong instructional skills demonstrated by the faculty, five of seven instructional strategies targeted in the Title I plan were being implemented in one or more classrooms.

Table 3. Middleville Elementary School: Average Scores on the CET

Indicator by Domain	Avg
Instructional Domain	3.0
Uses techniques which develop the lesson effectively	3.0
Sequences lesson to promote learning	3.3
Uses available materials to achieve lesson objectives	3.1
Adjusts lesson when appropriate	2.8
Presents content at developmentally appropriate level	3.5
Presents accurate subject matter	3.7
Relates relevant examples ... or events to content	2.5
Accommodates individual differences	2.6
Communicates effectively with students	3.4
Stimulates and encourages higher order thinking	2.6
Encourages student participation	3.1
Monitors on-going performance of students	2.9
Provides feedback to students regarding their progress	2.9
Management Domain	3.1
Organizes space, materials,equipment to facilitate learning	3.2
Promotes a positive learning climate	3.2
Manages routines/transitions in timely manner	3.1
Manages/adjusts time for planned activities	3.0
Establishes expectations for learning behavior	3.3
Uses monitoring techniques to facilitate learning	3.1

Note.   Scores ranged from 1 = "Unsatisfactory" to 4 = "Demonstrates Excellence." Midpoint was 2.5.

Staff Development

Of the nine instructional strategies proposed in the Title I plan, seven strategies, illustrated in Table 4, were to be part of the teaching repertoire of the faculty. We found evidence from interviews with teachers and the principal that three of the seven strategies (hands-on strategies, teaching for multiple intelligences, and fostering students' higher order thinking), had been included in the staff development in which teachers participated.

Table 4.　Middleville Elementary School Comparison of Title I Instructional Strategies, Staff Development Provided, and Implementation Observed

Instructional Strategies Written into the Title I Plan	Staff Development Provided	Implementation Observed
Hands-on strategies	Yes (4)[a]	Yes (2)[b]
Computer assisted instruction	No	No
Thematic units	No	Yes (1)
Collaborative learning	No	Yes(1)
Multiple intelligences	Yes (1)	Yes (3)
Self-directed learning	No	No
Higher order thinking	Yes (4)	Yes (2)

[a]"Yes" indicates that staff development was provided. The numbers indicate how many teachers mentioned the activity during interviews.
[b]"Yes" indicates that implementation was observed. The numbers indicate the number of classrooms in which the strategy was observed.

Because neither a Title I plan nor a faculty's participation in staff development ensures that teachers will implement new teaching strategies, we included a column in Table 4 to recap which of the Title I instructional strategies were observed being implemented. Implementation was observed for each strategy for which staff development was provided, suggesting an important link between the two.

Teachers' attitudes about staff development were measured through items on the questionnaire. Teachers gave staff development at Middleville moderate to high marks. Most teachers (88%) agreed that staff development activities addressed skills that would enhance their teaching, and that the activities addressed issues of importance to them (76%). The quality of staff development was high, according to 52% of the teachers. The positive attitude teachers expressed toward staff development may have been due, in part, to their participation in determining the staff development activities. Nearly three-fourths of the teachers said they had input in planning staff development.

Leadership

<u>Principal's leadership style.</u> Ms. Logan appeared to have an open style of leadership and to be dedicated to providing a solid education to all the children at the school. She went to great lengths to ensure that the program for the gifted students did not overshadow or detract from the academic program of the regular students. She related an example, describing an "archeological find" in which regular students hid artifacts which the gifted students found. Alternatively, gifted students would initiate an activity to which the regular students responded. Not only would students in the two programs confer about such activities, but also this strategy integrated both groups of children in interesting activities that were academic in nature.

In her three years at the school, Ms. Logan established an esprit de corps among the teachers that paid dividends in the perceptions of teachers. Twenty-five of the 34 teachers who made comments on the questionnaire described the Title I schoolwide program under Ms. Logan's leadership as "very effective," noting that student interest in learning had increased and that teachers used a wider variety of instructional strategies. One teacher wrote, "I am not certain how [the Title I program] affects test scores, but I have seen big improvements in the work and attitudes of students." Ms. Logan did not credit herself with the improvements, rather she said the strengths of the Title I program at Middleville were the openness of the faculty, their interest in looking at data critically, and their willingness to try different strategies to find what worked for the students.

Ms. Logan's leadership resulted in positive responses from teachers on the teacher questionnaire. Nearly all teachers felt that instructional time was protected at the school (92%), and that the principal supported their efforts to improve student achievement

(80%).   Teachers also thought the principal did a good job of getting resources for the school (95%).

School Climate at Middleville

The principal and the teachers.   On the questionnaire, Ms. Logan marked that she "strongly agreed" that the school was safe for students and staff. She "strongly agreed" that the discipline policy was enforced consistently, and that teachers received administrative support with discipline problems.

Teachers also perceive the school to be safe for students and staff (100%). Teachers differed somewhat with the principal about consistent enforcement of discipline policy and about administrative support when discipline problems arose, though three-fourths felt that these were not problematic issues. Teachers' overall impression of the school climate was strongly positive. Of the 34 who responded to open-ended items on the questionnaire, 29 characterized the school climate as positive, family-like, and/or caring.

The students.   Students saw the school in a positive light as well. Nearly all agreed the school was safe for students (93%) and most agreed that students followed class rules (75%) . These perceptions are consistent with those of the observers, who noted few disciplinary problems in classrooms.

Students were asked to name the three best and worst things about Middleville. The "teachers" were named one of the best things by 40 students; recess and other academic breaks followed as a distant second with 15 mentions. The principal, mentioned by few students at other schools as one of the best things about a school, was named by 14 students as among the best things at Middleville. Students made comments about the principal such as, we "have the best principal ever," and, "Ms. [Logan] is very open-minded [and] is fun to be around." The faculty inspired student comments as well, including, "Awesome teachers," and, "If I have a problem, the teachers or an adult can solve it," and, we have "the best teachers who care about your learning."

One of the worst things about Middleville, according to 19 students, was the poor condition of the school and bathrooms. One student wrote, "[Middleville] school is falling down." Opinions were mixed about the condition of the school, however. Some students named the appearance of the school as one of the best things, noting an appreciation of the gardens and courtyard, commenting that the school was "nice and clean," and that they liked "how they fix up the eating room on the holidays." Students who misbehave, curse, and talk back to teachers were named by 11 students as one of the worst things; fighting and getting punished were each named by seven students as one of the worst things about the school. Fifteen students made no negative comments or wrote a comment like the following, "I think there isn't any problem. I think this facility is one of the best schools in the [district]." This level of student satisfaction was rare across the 30 schools studied.

Summary

Middleville Elementary developed a grass roots approach to school improvement, which paid off. Not only were student test scores higher than would be expected for the population served, but both the professional staff and students found the school a pleasant place to be. Although much of the instruction was directed toward skill building and drill activities, inroads were being made to implement more engaging instructional strategies.

Rivertown Elementary School

General Characteristics

Rivertown Elementary School, which served approximately 620 students in SY 1998-99, was a bit larger than Middleville. Both schools, however, were attended by students in pre-kindergarten through fifth grade, and by SY 1998-99, had participated in the Title I schoolwide program for at least 3 years.

Rivertown served an impoverished population from one of the most economically deprived areas in the city. The campus has a distinct inner-city, urban atmosphere. According to data in the Title I plan, 82% of the students at Rivertown were considered economically deprived, up from 76% the prior year. Also, 86% of the students described themselves as African American, 11% as white, and 3% as other. As with Middleville, many of the students who were not African-American were in a gifted program that the district placed at the school for the purpose of attracting white students.

During SY 1998-99, there was considerable instability in the student body, as had been the case for several years. Only 49% of third through fifth graders indicated that they had attended Rivertown for three or more years. This is a marked contrast to Middleville where 73% of the student body had attended the school for at least three years.

The faculty at Rivertown, on the other hand, was more stable than the Middleville faculty. Approximately 57% of the Rivertown faculty had been at the school for less than five years, while 13% had been at the school for more than 10 years. The principal, Ms. Albert, had been at the school for less than five years.

Scores on the ITBS for third grade students at Rivertown in the Spring 1999 were lower than those at Middleville, but were up from the prior year. Rivertown third graders scored at the 38th percentile in reading, language scores were at the 32nd percentile, math scores were at the 47th percentile; and the composite total for the battery was at the 43rd percentile. The math score reflects a 17 percentage point increase over the prior year.

Scores for Rivertown fifth graders were slightly higher. In reading, fifth graders scored at the 40th percentile, in language at the 50th percentile, in math at the 44th percentile, and composite total was at the 43rd percentile. As mentioned, nearly all scores for both grade levels were up from the previous year (SY 1997-98). The overall composite scores for Rivertown and Middleville at the third grade level were about the same, while Middleville scored higher (53rd percentile) than Rivertown (43rd percentile) on the fifth grade composite score.

Scores on the state administered CRT were not as good. Fourth graders at Rivertown did much worse than their peers at Middleville and statewide. Only 37% of the Rivertown students scored at the basic, proficient, or advanced levels on the English/Language Arts section of the CRT, and only 26% of the students scored at these levels on the mathematics section of the CRT. Our data do not explain why third and fifth graders would score near the 50th percentile on the ITBS, but fourth graders would do so poorly on the state CRT.

Title I Plan and Its Implementation at Rivertown

According to the Title I plan for Rivertown, the school received $557,289, well over a half a million dollars, in Title I funds for the three years spanning FY 1996-97 to FY 1998-99 (K. T. Associates, 2000). For FY 1998-99, 63% of the Title I budget was spent on personnel. Altogether nearly $50,000 was spent on the Success for All (SFA) program in FY 1998-99, including personnel costs and contractual services.

Like Middleville, Rivertown established two goals in its Title I plan that addressed instruction and staff development. To achieve these goals, six strategies that related to instruction, and six that related to staff development were developed. Table 5 lists these goals and strategies. A comparison with Table 1, where information about the Middleville plan can be found, indicates some similarities. The main difference between the schools, as noted earlier, is that Rivertown adopted the SFA program, while Middleville developed its own strategies for school improvement.

Table 5. Rivertown Elementary School: Title I Instructional Goals and Related Strategies for Implementation Goals

Goals
1. Increase academic achievement in language arts and mathematics
2. Increase parent involvement
Instruction
1. Success for All Program
2. Thematic units/Interdisciplinary instruction
3. Multi-age grouping
4. Computer assisted instruction
5. Accelerated Reader Program
6. Reading strategies
Staff Development Topics
1. Success for All
2. Computer use
3. Accelerated Reader
4. Reading strategies
5. Authentic assessment
6. Test Taking Skills

Comments on the Title I plan. We focus our discussion in this chapter on the instructional and staff development components of the Title I plans at these two schools because those components most directly affect the instructional core. Nevertheless, a few comments are in order regarding the overall scope of Rivertown Title I plan. We make this deviation because we feel the breadth of the plan constrained the accomplishment of some of the instructional and staff development components.

The Title I plan at Rivertown contained five programs that competed with one another for resources. These programs included: (a) the SFA program, which received the most resources, (b) the Accelerated Reader program, (c) a computer assisted instruction component, (d) a reading strategies component, and (e) a schoolwide discipline program that included a social worker. The district contributed to the multiplicity of programs at Rivertown by placing the gifted program at the school.

The complexity of the plan, we believe, created a degree of fragmentation that affected the overall implementation. During an interview, Ms. Albert noted that the three most important components of the Title I program were SFA, computerized assisted instruction, and the schoolwide discipline program. These components were also most frequently named by the eight interviewed teachers. However, several of the teachers could not speak in detail about these components. This appeared to be primarily a function of the fragmentation, not teachers' disregard for the Title I program.

In a similar vein, the gifted program caused some strain that affected the coherence of the schoolwide program. Ms. Albert noted that only eight of the 60 gifted students were from the neighborhood. She explained that this ratio was important because Rivertown had recently experienced a change in attendance boundaries, and thus student body composition, in order to become a "neighborhood" school. The district office required that gifted students be separated from the rest of the student body except for extra-curricular activities, recess, and lunch. As a result of the staff's perceptions of this mandate, no efforts were made at Rivertown to integrate the two programs. Compounding the difficulties, teachers in the regular program were unhappy that the gifted students enjoyed a small pupil-teacher ratio, while neighborhood youngsters were in classes with two to three times as many students. This disparity was seen as an inequity by some teachers and by Ms. Albert, who contended that the effect of the gifted program was to siphon resources away from the neighborhood children, rather than to benefit them.

Instructional goals and strategies. Table 6 shows the extent to which components of the Title I plan were seen in nine classroom observations. The most frequently observed components were SFA and multi-age grouping, which occurred as a result of SFA. These were observed in the five SFA classes that were visited. Thematic units, use of computers, and the Accelerated Reader Program were not observed in any classroom.

Table 6. Rivertown Elementary School: Instructional Strategies in Title I Plan and Number of Times Strategy Observed in Classrooms

Program components	Times observed
Success for All	5
Thematic units	0
Multi-age grouping	5[a]
Computers in use	0
Accelerated Reader Program	0
Other Observed Attributes	
Higher order thinking skills	0
Knowledge/skill building/drill	9
Strong academic press	2
Effective classroom management	4
Positive classroom climate	5
Weak academic press	4
Ineffective classroom management	2
Negative classroom climate	2

NOTE: Observations occurred in 9 classrooms, including 5 when SFA was taught.
[a]Multi-age grouping was observed only in the 5 SFA classes.

Lessons in all nine classes were primarily oriented toward skill building and drill activities; higher order thinking skills were not observed in any class. In two classes, however, a strong academic press was evident. Effective classroom management strategies were observed in four classes, and a positive climate was noted in five classes. As happened at Middleville, in the two classes in which academic press was strong, the teachers were also effective managers and warm toward students. These findings point out that teacher warmth and effective class management do not necessarily result in strong academic press. Academic press is a third skill which teachers must employ to maximize student learning.

In comparison to Middleville, teaching at Rivertown was somewhat less effective. For example, weak academic press was observed in four classes where frequent off-task behavior went uncorrected or where student learning appeared ancillary to moving through written lesson plans. Ineffective classroom management was noted in two classes in which teachers were unable to control student misbehavior despite persistent efforts. Two classes were observed in which classroom climate was negative.

SFA was the main focus of the Title I plan at Rivertown, therefore, special note will be made regarding the implementation of SFA. To document the SFA program, five classroom observations were conducted during the time SFA strategies were being used. Reading activities were similar across age levels. Students were assigned to classes by instructional level, not grade level, provided a three year age span was not exceeded. During the ninety minute block set aside for SFA, teachers implemented several SFA strategies. For example, teachers read to students and asked factual questions about the plot, characters, or relevant historical events. Teachers also engaged students in vocabulary development and had students sound out words they could not readily read.

Teachers seemed pleased with the progress students made through SFA. Even teachers who felt their creativity was stifled by the program commented that as a result of SFA, students were now reading for pleasure and were better, more independent, more confident readers. Given that test scores were up over the prior year, the program seemed to be having a positive impact. This accomplishment takes on greater meaning in light of the turnover of the student body.

Teachers' Classroom Performance at Rivertown

Time-on-task (TOT) was low at Rivertown. Interactive TOT was 36%, compared to 61% for Middleville. Total TOT was 47%, compared to 68% for Middleville. One cause for low TOT at Rivertown was the number of interruptions from visitors, tardy students, and the intercommunication system, that occurred during the observations. These interruptions varied from none to three during 30 minute observations, with a mode of one interruption per observation time period, an unacceptably high rate.

CET data, which are presented in Table 7, corroborate the scripting data and indicate that Rivertown teachers were less skilled than those at Middleville. The average score for the instructional indicators for Rivertown teachers was 2.7, while Middleville teachers averaged 3.0. The indicators on which Rivertown teachers scored an average of 3 or above were: presents accurate subject matter (3.1), presents content at a developmentally appropriate level (3.0), and encourages student participation (3.0).

On the other hand, teachers scored lowest on stimulating and encouraging higher order thinking (2.2) and adjusting the lesson when appropriate (2.4). Here, the scores are below the "2.5" mid-point of the range. CET data regarding higher order thinking support the other classroom observation data, helping to confirm that opportunities for higher order thinking were not a significant part of instruction at Rivertown.

The average score for the management indicators at Rivertown was 2.7, as compared to Middleville where the average was 3.1. Rivertown teachers scored above 3.0 on one indicator, organizes space, materials, and equipment to facilitate learning (3.1). The lowest scores were at the mid-point of the range, and included the indicators manages routines/transitions in a timely manner (2.5); establishes expectations for learning behavior (2.5); and uses monitoring techniques to facilitate learning (2.5).

Table 7. Rivertown Elementary School: Average Scores on CET

Indicator by Domain	Avg
Instructional Domain	2.7
Uses techniques which develop lesson effectively	2.6
Sequences lesson to promote learning	2.7
Uses available materials to achieve lesson objectives	2.6
Adjusts lesson when appropriate	2.4
Presents content at developmentally appropriate level	3.0
Presents accurate subject matter	3.1
Relates relevant examples ... or events to content	2.8
Accommodates individual differences	2.5
Communicates effectively with students	2.8
Stimulates and encourages higher order thinking	2.2
Encourages student participation	3.0
Monitors on-going performance of students	2.6
Provides feedback to students regarding their progress	2.6
Management Domain	2.7
Organizes space, materials, equipment to facilitate learning	3.1
Promotes a positive learning climate	2.7
Manages routines/transitions in timely manner	2.5
Manages/adjusts time for planned activities	2.6
Establishes expectations for learning behavior	2.5
Uses monitoring techniques to facilitate learning	2.5

Note. Scores ranged from 1='Unsatisfactory' to 4 ='Demonstrates Excellence.'
Midpoint was 2.5.

In summary, the scores of Rivertown teachers on the classroom observation instruments were lower than those obtained by the Middleville teachers. Nonetheless, both interview and observation data suggest that teachers at Rivertown were working toward school improvement with some success. Scores were up on the ITBS, and the SFA program was being implemented. Additional staff development was needed, however, particularly to assist teachers in honing techniques for fostering student's higher order thinking. In addition to the instructional aspects of the Title I plan, there was evidence that the discipline program was having a positive effect. However, CET data indicated that staff development was still needed to improve classroom management skills.

Staff Development

Expenditures related to SFA were calculated as part of the staff development effort. Through a budget analysis, we estimated that approximately $59,200, was allocated for staff development for the three years FY 1996-97 through FY 1998-99. This allocation amounts to 11% of the total three year budget and is substantially more than the .5% to 3% that was allocated by other schools involved in our multi-year study of schoolwide programs (K.T. Associates, 1997, 1998, 2000).

Table 8 focuses on the relationship between instructional strategies included in the Title I plan, staff development, and implementation. The instructional strategies proposed in the schoolwide Title I plan are listed in the first column on the table. The second column indicates the staff development activities that were actually provided, according to interviewed teachers. There is substantial correspondence between the instructional strategies proposed in the Title I plan and the staff development provided. The only instructional strategy for which no staff development was provided was the Accelerated Reader Program. The third column indicates which of the instructional strategies were observed being implemented. Here a breakdown occurs. The only strategies observed during the class visits were SFA, multi-age grouping, and reading strategies other than SFA.

Table 8. Rivertown Elementary School Comparison of Title I Instructional Strategies, Staff Development Provided, and Implementation Observed

Instructional Strategies Proposed for Implementation	Staff Development Provided	Implementation Observed
Success For All	Yes (5)[a]	Yes (5)[b]
Thematic units	Through SFA (1)	No
Multi-age grouping	Through SFA (1)	Yes (5)
Computer assisted instruction	Yes (2)	No
Accelerated Reader Program	No	No
Reading strategies	Yes (2)	Yes
Test taking	Yes (3)	N/O[c]

[a] "Yes"indicates that staff development was provided. The numbers indicate how many teachers mentioned the activity during interviews.
[b] "Yes" indicates that implementation was observed. The numbers indicated the number of classrooms in which the strategy was observed.
[c] "N/O" indicates the strategy was not observable.

All eight teachers who were interviewed mentioned being involved in staff development activities. The most widely mentioned training involved SFA, which was noted by five teachers. The next most frequently mentioned instructional strategies were computer-assisted instruction and reading strategies, which were each named by two teachers.

Teachers also mentioned participating in staff development that was not directly related to instruction. A primary goal of the district was to raise test scores. To support this goal, the district required teachers to attend training about teaching test taking skills to students. A second in-service activity mentioned by three teachers was classroom management/student discipline. According to several interviewed teachers, discipline had improved as a result. With a few notable exceptions, classroom observations confirmed that discipline problems were seldom the cause of class interruptions.

Although Rivertown teachers were involved in staff development activities, when compared to Middleville teachers they were not particularly positive about their experiences. This finding was a surprise because much of the staff development activities at the school were through SFA. About two-thirds of the Rivertown teachers (compared to 88% at Middleville) agreed that staff development addressed skills that would enhance their teaching, and 59% agreed that the training activities were about issues that were important to them (compared to 76% at Middleville). Perhaps because most of the in-service activities were mandated either by SFA or by the district, only 43% marked that staff development activities were planned with teacher input (compared to 72% at Middleville). The most troubling finding regarding staff development was that only 39% of the teachers thought the staff development activities at Rivertown were better than at other schools (compared to 52% at Middleville).

Leadership at Rivertown
   Principal's leadership style. Like Ms. Logan at Middleville, responses to questionnaire items concerning Ms. Albert's leadership style were quite positive. In the opinion of most teachers, Ms. Albert supported their efforts to improve student achievement (88%), and did a good job of getting resources for the school (96%). Teachers also felt that instructional time was protected by Ms. Albert, with 92% expressing this opinion, although as mentioned previously, research team members did not share this perception. Finally, all of the teachers responding to the questionnaire indicated that Ms. Albert involved them in the school improvement process (100%) and 92% said they were involved in decision making regarding the development of school policies on a regular basis.

   Notwithstanding faculty perceptions, other data suggest some leadership weaknesses. One problem area was the feelings of some faculty and Ms. Albert about the gifted program. Ms. Albert took issue with policies that allocated resources, such as a low pupil-teacher ratio, to a program that involved so few children from the school's catchment area. While her position is understandable, she did not describe any proactive efforts to intermingle students from the two programs, as happened at Middleville, an effort that might have redistributed some of the resources to the benefit of the neighborhood children.

Another problem, raised by Ms. Albert, was that some teachers were not committed to SFA, feeling that their creativity was stifled by the program. Although the research team did not uncover strong feelings of dissatisfaction with SFA, some teachers did not fully endorse the program. This ambivalence may have had several sources. One could be the several competing programs included in the Title I plan, as discussed above. Teachers who wished to have more control of their teaching than is available with SFA may have been attracted to one of the other programs in the plan, only to find it beyond their reach. Another source of ambivalence could be that the school had a senior staff many of whom held graduate degrees. These veteran teachers are more likely than new teachers to be unsupportive of an externally developed program. For her part, Ms. Albert strongly endorsed SFA and expressed concerned about the ambivalence of these faculty members; however, she also did not describe any strategy for dealing with the issue.

School Climate

The principal and the teachers. Ms. Albert's opinions about school climate differed from those of the teachers and students. On the questionnaire, she indicated that the school was safe for students and staff, and the discipline policy was enforced consistently. She also indicated "strong" agreement that administrators were supportive of teachers when discipline problems arose.

Teachers, on the other hand, were more conservative in their assessment on each of the above counts. For example, 75% of Rivertown teachers agreed that the school was safe for students, though 81% agreed the campus was safe for staff. Issues about student safety may result from the community in which the school was located. At Rivertown, 63% of teachers marked that the discipline policy was consistently enforced, compared to 74% of Middleville. Teachers at the two school were similar in their opinions about administrative support with disciplinary problems, with 75% and 73% of the teachers, respectively at Rivertown and Middleville, agreeing they were supported.

The students. The opinions of Rivertown students were more similar to those of the teachers than of the principal regarding school safety. Of the third, fourth, and fifth graders who completed questionnaires, 74% agreed that the school was safe for them, a perception very similar to that of the teachers. Many Rivertown students (83%) said they knew the rules for good behavior, but 76% agreed that students often disrupted class.

The opinions of students about misbehavior were reflected in open-ended items on the questionnaire as well. As occurred at Middleville, the youngsters were asked to name the three best and worst things about their school. Most frequently named as best were lunch, recess, and physical education, with 29 students noting these breaks from class as one of the best things about the school. However, a very close second was learning and specific subjects, particularly music, which were named by 28 students as one of the best things. Thus, students at both schools felt that some aspect of the academic program was among the best things about school. Teachers were named by 15 Rivertown students as among the best things at school. Affection for the faculty prompted such student comments as, "One of the best things about my school is my teacher!" and, "They [the teachers] let us do fun things."

To the students, the worst thing about Rivertown was fighting and student misbehavior, an opinion expressed by 26 students. Several students made comments like, "We need to stop fighting," and, "Students threaten and fight other students," and, "Cuss words – I hear them every day." In the same vein, 15 students said "mean kids" were among the worst things about Rivertown. Such comments reinforce teachers' and students' reservations about school safety. The third most commonly named "worst thing" about the school was the poor overall condition of the buildings, particularly the bathrooms. Sixteen students cited this problem, with one writing the comment, "Old, smelly, and dirty bathrooms. Peeling paint," while another wrote, "Not very nice looking or clean." The physical conditions of the Rivertown facility are a contrast with Middleville where some students complained that the buildings were old while others praised the attractiveness of the grounds.

Summary
Rivertown Elementary adopted Success for All as the major component of its Title I schoolwide plan. Teachers seemed pleased, in general, with the progress the students were making in reading through SFA. Despite scores on state administered CRTs that were low, especially in mathematics, the ITBS results were an

improvement over the prior year but were higher than found at most schools in the multiyear study. Observations in classrooms indicated that teacher performance in both the instructional and management areas were in an acceptable range and could be improved even more with targeted staff development.

Comparative Case Study Analysis

The two schools are very similar on several important context variables. Table 9 compares Middleville and Rivertown Elementary Schools on a variety of dimensions. They are located in the same district, serve the same type of community, have the same grade configuration, serve approximately the same number of students, and have approximately the same percentage of students on the free lunch program. The percentage of African-American students at Middleville was somewhat lower than at Rivertown, but both schools served primarily African-American communities. The only two context variables on which the schools differed were the stability of student body, which was more stable at Middleville, and the stability of faculty, which was more stable at Rivertown. Thus, the two schools are exceptionally well matched on context variables.

Differences between the schools occurred with regard to three categories of variables; the Title I program, leadership of the principal, and outcomes. One of the most important differences between the two schools was the nature of the schoolwide program itself. Middleville developed its own schoolwide program, shaping and modifying it to accommodate the students who attended the school. Rivertown, on the other hand, adopted a Special Strategy, Success for All, that has a strong research base that indicates the program was appropriate for the characteristics of the majority students who attended the school.

Because the type of programs differed, so did allocations from the Title I budgets. At Middleville, budgetary allocations went primarily to instructional materials, while the Rivertown budget emphasized salaries and contracts needed for the implementation of the SFA program. Interestingly, the schools also differed with regard to staff development. Despite the nationally recognized Special Strategy at Rivertown, staff development was rated higher by the Middleville faculty. Our data indicate two possible causes. One cause was the "louder voice" given to the

Middleville faculty in determining staff development activities. The second was the ambivalence of some Rivertown faculty for SFA, which may have cause less enthusiasm for the associated staff development.

Table 9. Dimensions of Contrast between Middleville and Rivertown Elementary Schools

Dimensions of Contrast	Middleville Elemen. School	Rivertown Elemen. School
Contextual Variables		
School district	Large district in the South	Same district
Community type	Urban	Urban
Grade level configuration	PK-5	PK-5
Number of students served	570	621
Poverty indicator	83% on free lunch program	82% on free lunch program
Ethnic make- up: African-American White Other	77% 20% 3%	86% 11% 3%
Stability of student body	More Stable: 72% attended for 3+ years	Less Stable: 49% attended for 3+ years:
Stability of faculty	Less Stable: 77% had 5 or fewer years	More Stable: 57% had 5 or fewer years
Title I Program Variables		
Type of Title I program	School generated	Special Strategies (SFA)

Dimensions of Contrast	Middleville Elemen. School	Rivertown Elemen. School
Years in schoolwide program	At least 3 years	At least 3 years
Focus of Title I budget	80% of FY 1998-99 budget allocated to materials 9% of budget allocated to salaries: math specialist hired	63% of FY 1998-99 budget allocated to salaries; Emphasis on SFA personnel and contracts
Staff development	Rated high by faculty	Rated moderate by faculty
Leadership and Leadership Influence Variables		
Principal's tenure at school	Less than 5 years	Less than 5 years
Principal's leadership	Strong and focused	Not as strong or focused
School climate	Warm and supportive	Generally warm, but some areas of concern
Teaching performance	Stronger: 68% time-on-task; Overall CET score of 3.0	Weaker: 47% time-on-task; Overall CET score of 2.7
Outcomes		
Degree of implementation of Title I program	Moderate/High	Varies by component from High to Low
Scores on achievement tests	High for population served; 4th grade CRT scores exceed state average	Average to low for population served; 4th grade CRT scores well below state average

A second category of variance between the two schools was principal leadership. The principals at both schools had less than five years tenure at the respective schools, and both were liked by the teachers. Ms. Logan at Middleville, however, appeared to the research team to be a more skillful leader, more focused on the schoolwide program, and more energetic about creating a supportive environment for both faculty and students. Her efforts, in turn, seemed to result in a warmer, more supportive learning climate for students. Because of Ms. Logan's attention to the instructional aspects of the Title I program, both time-on-task and teaching quality were higher than at Rivertown.

Ms. Albert at Rivertown, on the other hand, was trying to implement a multifaceted schoolwide program. The complexity of the program seemed to divide her attention among its many components and, as a result, some managerial responsibilities, such as limiting the interruption of instructional time, got less notice. Nonetheless, Ms. Albert was able to promote a generally warm climate in most classrooms, as well as adequate, though not exemplary, teaching.

The third category in which the two schools differed was outcomes. One outcome was the degree of implementation of the Title I program. A second, and we suggest, related, outcome was achievement scores. Perhaps because of the more "hands-on" involvement of the Middleville faculty in shaping the schoolwide program, the degree of implementation was moderate to high. By contrast, program implementation at Rivertown varied by component from low to high. Part of this variation at Rivertown was likely due to the complex set of components included in the Title I plan. Another contributor was that some of the faculty were not fully supporting SFA, thus, effectiveness differed from teacher to teacher.

These differences, taken together, help to explain why Middleville students scored higher on achievement tests, especially the 4th grade CRTs, than the Rivertown students. Had Ms. Albert been a more skillful leader, she may been able to overcome the ambivalence of some teachers to SFA, resulting in more attentive involvement in staff development, greater fidelity to the teaching techniques emphasized in SFA, and higher reading scores. She might also have included fewer components in the Title I plan, but more emphasis on mathematics to address the low scores in that area.

Conclusions

The purpose of this chapter is to investigate Title I schoolwide programs that were achieving some success. The similarity of the schools on a number of contextual and demographic variables allows for interesting comparisons. One conclusion is that the "home grown" program being implemented at Middleville resulted in better outcomes than the "off-the-shelf" Special Strategies approach adopted at Rivertown. Our study indicates that the Special Strategies approach is not a panacea and does not guarantee that teacher behavior in the classroom will change, as Teddlie and Meza have pointed out elsewhere (1999). Other variables must be present, such as the commitment of all of the faculty. The data, however, also suggest at least two other conclusions as well.

Our research on Title I schoolwide programs has taught us that programs are more likely to be implemented if they are internally consistent. That is, the components of the plan are mutually complementary and staff development tracks the instructional strategies targeted for implementation. At Middleville, the use of hands-on strategies, multiple intelligences, and teaching for higher order thinking were complementary instructional strategies included in the Title I plan; teachers participated in staff development regarding these strategies, and implementation was observed. At Rivertown, the multiplicity of plan components competed for resources, including teachers' attention. While staff development was provided, it appeared to be of lesser quality. As a result of these two variables, implementation was less effective at Rivertown.

A second conclusion that explains the differences in program effectiveness is principal leadership. Both principals in this study had approximately the same years of administrative experience, eliminating experience as a variable. Ms. Logan's skill as a leader enabled her to maintain a focus on implementing strategies that allowed the children who attended Middleville to learn successfully. A less skillful leader, Ms. Albert allowed a complex program to be promulgated in the face of inconsistent faculty support and struggled with implementation of the multiple components with less success.

References

David, J. (1991) . What it takes to restructure education. *Educational Leadership, 48* (8), 11-15.

Elmore, R. (1995). Structured reform and educational practice. *Educational Researcher, 24* (9), 23-26.

Fullan, M. (1993). *Change forces: Probing the depths of educational reform.* London: Falmer.

Hallinger, P. and Murphy, J. (1986) The social context of effective schools. *American Journal of Education, 94,* 328-355.

Keller, B.M., & & Soler, P. (1994). *The influence of the Accelerated schools philosophy and process on classroom practices.* Paper presented at the Annual Meeting of the American Educational Research Association.

K. T. Associates (1997). *Cross-site case study analysis: East Baton Rouge Parish School System Title I Program, School Year 1996-97.* Baton Rouge, LA: Author.

K. T. Associates (1998). *Cross-site case study analysis: East Baton Rouge Parish School System Title I Program, School Year 1997-98.* Baton Rouge, LA: Author.

K. T. Associates (2000). *Cross-site case study analysis: East Baton Rouge Parish School System Title I Program, School Year 1998-99.* Baton Rouge, LA: Author.

Reynolds, D., Teddlie, C., Hopkins, D. and Stringfield, S. (2000). School effectiveness and school improvement. In C. Teddlie and D. Reynolds (Eds.) *The international handbook of school effectiveness research,* pp. 206-231. London: Falmer Press.

Spradley, J. P. (1979). *The ethnographic interview.* New York: Holt, Rinehart and Winston.

Spradley, J. P. (1980). *Participant observation.* New York: Holt, Rinehart and Winston.

Stallings, J. (1980). Allocated academic learning time revisited, or beyond time on task. *Educational Researcher, 9*(11), 11-16.

Stringfield, S., Winfield, L., and Abt Associates, Inc. (1994) *Urban and suburban/rural special strategies for educating disadvantaged children: First year report.* Washington, D.C. : U.S. Department of Education.

Stringfield, S., Millsap, M. A. and Herman, R. (1997) *Urban and suburban/rural special strategies for educating disadvantaged children: Findings and policy implications of a longitudinal study.*

Washington DC : US Department of Education.

Tashakkori, A., and Teddlie, C. (1998). *Mixed methodology: Combining the qualitative and quantitative approaches.* Thousand Oaks, CA: Sage Publications, Inc.

Taylor, D. L. & Teddlie, C. (1992). *Restructuring and the classroom: A view from a reform district.* Paper presented at the annual meeting of the American Educational Research Association, San Francisco, CA.

Taylor, D. L. & Teddlie, C. (1992). *Restructuring without changing: Constancy in the classroom in a restructured district.* Paper presented at the annual meeting of the American Educational Research Association, San Francisco.

Taylor, D. L. & Teddlie, C. (1998). *An intensive process/product evaluation of Title I schoolwide implementation.* Paper presented at the annual meeting of the American Educational Research Association, San Diego, CA.

Taylor, D. L. & Teddlie, C. (1999a). *Evaluating the effects of Title 1 schoolwide programs at the elementary, middle, and high school levels.* Paper presented at the annual meeting of the American Educational Research Association, Montreal, Canada.

Taylor, D. L. & Teddlie, C. (1999b) Implementation fidelity in Title I schoolwide programs. *Journal of Education for Students Placed At Risk., 4,* 299-319.

Teddlie, C., Kochan, S., & Taylor, D. L. (2000, April). *ABC+: Variations on a context-sensitive model for school performance measurement and school improvement.* Paper presented at the annual meeting of the American Educational Research Association, New Orleans, LA.

Teddlie, C., and Meza, J. (1999) Using informal and formal measures to create classroom profiles. In J. Freiberg (Ed.) *School climate: Measuring, improving and sustaining healthy learning environments*, pp. 77-99. London: Falmer Press.

Teddlie, C. and Stringfield, S. (1993) *Schools make a difference : Lessons learned from a 10-year study of school effects.* New York : Teachers College Press.

Yin, R. K. (1994). *Case study research design and methods.* (2nd. ed.). Newbury Park, CA: Sage Publication.

CHAPTER 5

TOWARD SYSTEMIC REFORM IN HIGH-POVERTY SCHOOLS: TITLE I SCHOOLWIDE PROGRAMS IN TWO LARGE DISTRICTS

Kenneth K. Wong & Kimberley F. Alkins

Introduction

According to O'Day and Smith (1993) most systemic reform strategies share a common purpose: to upgrade significantly the quality of the curriculum and instruction delivered to all children. To accomplish this goal, the reforms require major changes in the way states and local school systems formulate and implement policy. Three changes characterize an idealized version of the model of systemic reform:

- *Curriculum frameworks* that establish what students should know and be able to do would provide direction and vision for significantly upgrading the quality of the content and instruction within all schools in the state.
- *Alignment of state and local education policies* would provide a coherent structure to support schools in designing effective strategies for teaching the content of the frameworks to all their students.
- *Restructured governance system* through which schools would have the resources, flexibility, and responsibility to design and implement effective strategies for preparing their students to learn the content of the curriculum frameworks to a high level of performance (O'Day and Smith, 1993, p. 251).

These high expectations for policy coherence are articulated at the federal, the state, and the district levels. In 1994, Congress adopted the Improving America's Schools Act (IASA), which established an ambitious agenda for systemic improvement in schools that serve students with at-risk backgrounds (commonly referred to as Title I schools). The legislation focused on utilizing schoolwide programs as a strategy to reduce curricular fragmentation and enhance instructional effectiveness in high poverty settings (Wong & Wang, 1994; Wang & Wong, 1997). These expectations were further strengthened by Public Law 105-78 enacted in November 1997 (known as the Obey-Porter legislation), in which Congress appropriated an additional $145 million to support the Comprehensive School Reform Demonstration program in high poverty Title I schools. Similar efforts to foster systemic reform have occurred in states and urban districts. While an increasing number of states have introduced more vigorous curriculum standards, many urban districts have developed strategies to improve low performing schools.

A key research question is the extent to which these high expectations are implemented in Title I schools with high at-risk populations. The literature in policy implementation clearly suggests that well-intended policy must negotiate through a complex institutional process in the multi-level educational system. District policy goals become loosely coupled at the school and classroom levels (Wong & Sunderman, 2000).

To understand the implementation of systemic reform in disadvantaged schools, we conducted case studies of Title I schoolwide programs in two large school districts, Montgomery County, Maryland and Philadelphia, Pennsylvania. The two districts not only have a substantial presence of children from poverty backgrounds, they have also made major efforts to improve academic standards districtwide. Montgomery County (Maryland) launched *Success for Every Student* in 1992, while Philadelphia began the *Children Achieving* reform in 1995.

We are interested in the impact of systemwide reforms on the following practices in Title I schoolwide programs: curriculum standards, assessment, professional development, and parental involvement. Further, we seek to understand how students, especially minority and low-income students, fare under a new reform initiative. In this chapter, we examine the implementation of these "systemic" features in selected Title I schoolwide programs in the two districts at (1) the systemwide level, (2) the school level and (3) classroom level. We also conduct preliminary analysis on student achievement trends in the two districts. This chapter is based on data collected for the Laboratory Network Program of the Regional Educational Laboratory Program led by the Laboratory for Student Success at Temple University.

Two Large School Districts in Perspective

One may ask how can we compare two school districts like Montgomery County and Philadelphia. Montgomery County, located on the border of the District of Columbia, is one of the largest counties in Maryland. Its population of 757,027 is affluent with a median household income of $59,652 and well-educated - of the persons 25 years and older, 90.6% have at least a high school diploma and 49.9% are college graduates. The population of Philadelphia (1,585,577) has a median household income of $26,854, with 64.3% of those 25 years and older holding a high school diploma but only 15.2% are college graduates. Even based on U.S. census poverty estimates, 5.4% of Montgomery County's population is in poverty versus 23.8% of Philadelphia's population (U.S. Census Bureau, 1996a, 1996b).

However, Montgomery County has a school system with many of the same problems facing older urban schools systems like Philadelphia. Jones and Hill (1997) state that Montgomery County has:

- an increasingly minority and poor student population with critical educational needs;
- a teaching staff that is not fully equipped or trained to effectively teach a diverse student population in the 1990s;
- less than adequate parental involvement, especially among poor and minority parents
- less than adequate infrastructure, i.e., overcrowded or deteriorated buildings;
- tight funding, especially in a period of increased demand (p. 2).

Additionally, in 1983 about one in eight students were eligible for the free and reduced-price meals program, while in 1997 one in four students were eligible for this program. In 1983 3,500 students enrolled in the English for Speakers of Other Languages (ESOL) program, while in 1997 the number had increased to 7,600, making the Montgomery County Public Schools (MCPS) system have over half of the ESOL students in the state (MCPS, 1998d, p. 7).

To address many of these problems and changing demographics, the MCPS adopted a new educational policy called *Success for Every Student* in 1992. The plan provides broad strategies, together with specific tasks, for schools, central administrative offices and other departments, parents and communities and was designed to concentrate attention on the achievement of specific outcome measures. Special and critical emphasis is placed upon addressing the needs of low- to average-achieving African American, Native American, Asian American and Latino students, as well as students with limited English proficiency and special needs. The strategies and tasks are organized to support four specific goals:

- Ensure Success for Every Student;
- Provide an Effective Instructional Program;
- Strengthen Productive Partnerships for Education;
- Create a Positive Work Environment in a Self-renewing organization.

Three years later in 1995 Superintendent David Hornbeck introduced the *Children Achieving* agenda to the Philadelphia School District. The *Children Achieving* Action Design charts a four and one-half year course that is organized around ten components that are similar to the goals, strategies and outcomes of the *Success for Every Student* plan. Philadelphia hopes to be the first urban school system to have *all* of its children succeed.

Research Design

This study gathered three kinds of information: (1) school-level data by interviewing twice during the academic year district-level administrators, principals, and teachers from selected sites that are implementing Title I reforms; (2) student-level data, including individual achievement test scores in reading and mathematics and socioeconomic data; and (3) district-level information on the implementation of Title I programs and reforms initiatives.

Research staff made site visits to schoolwide program sites in Philadelphia and Montgomery County and collected school and classroom data on the implementation and effect of reform on

Title I schoolwide programs. At each site, project staff interviewed and/or surveyed the principal, program coordinators for Title I services, reading specialists, instructional aides, and classroom teachers. Classroom observations were also conducted. Particular attention was given to instructional practices, curriculum, and resource allocation patterns. Project staff also reviewed other efforts by the school staff to improve academic achievement, including better coordination of Title I resources and other categorical funds. Each participating school was scheduled for a day-long site visitation.

Student-level data includes individual test scores in reading and mathematics, socioeconomic data, and participation in Title I programs for all elementary students in the district. In addition, we reviewed the district's public documents on federal Title I, briefly interviewed district administrators about Title I programs, and gathered information on Title I program funding.

Data Collection

In 1997, we began studying three elementary schools (MacLeod, Martin, Morgan)[1] in Montgomery County that have implemented Title I schoolwide programs since 1995. Martin has a predominately African American and Latino population, Morgan and MacLeod have a predominately Latino population.

In 1996, four inner-city Philadelphia elementary schools (Parkland, Paine, Pine Crest, Phillips), each one from a different cluster, were selected. Selection was based on socio-economic characteristics of the schools to represent the diversity in Philadelphia's School District.[2] Phillips has a predominately Latino population, Pine Crest has a significant Asian population. And the two remaining schools are predominately African American.

Background Information

Table 1 provides detailed information about the schools and districts.[3] Information is also provided about state enrollment. During the 1997-98 school year MCPS had 184 schools and Philadelphia had 259 schools. It is important to note that, overall, the three schools in Montgomery County have a significantly higher special services population, with the exception of percent special education, than the district and the state of Maryland. Additionally, while whites make up over 50% of the district and state school population, they make up approximately 7.8% of the student population at Martin, 15.4% of the population at Morgan, and 12.2% of the population at MacLeod. These percentages are more representative of the school population in Philadelphia. However, based on physical appearance and available resources the schools in Philadelphia are much more "disadvantaged" than the schools in MCPS. Further, based on 1996 fiscal data provided by the National Center for Education Statistics (NCES) Philadelphia's per pupil expenditure was $2,468 less than that of MCPS (NCES, 1999). This can be explained by the fact that a majority (approximately 80%) of MCPS revenues come from the local government compared to Philadelphia's 40% and, as stated in the beginning of this section, the median income in Montgomery County is $59,000 opposed to Philadelphia's $26,000. Stated simply, Montgomery County is a wealthier school district.

Overall, Montgomery County's schools are far more racially integrated than schools in the nation as a whole; and the average student achievement for all racial groups exceeds national averages. However, there is a continuing disparity between the school performance of some African American, Latino and Native American and Asian American and white students. The overall achievement of the students in the three MCPS schools is significantly lower than that of the district. We will explore these disparities later in the paper.

Title I Programs
In order to analyze the impact of the reform initiatives on the schools, it is necessary to understand the scope, goals, and operations of the federal Title I schoolwide programs in Montgomery County and Philadelphia.

In the Philadelphia School District, a majority of the schools are Title I schools. Presently, two-thirds of all of Philadelphia's 259 schools receive Title I funding. During the 1996-1997 school year, the schools collectively received 78.9 million dollars in federal Title I funding to employ 1,900 staff persons to provide instructional and support services to over 131,000 students (School District of Philadelphia, n.d. 3).

Table 1a. School Information Select Schools, School Districts and States, 1997-1998.

| | Montgomery County, Maryland | | | | |
| | Schools | | | District | State |
	Martin	Morgan	MacLeod	Montgomery Co.	Maryland
Student Enrollment	345	778	549	125,023	830,744
Grade Levels	3-6	PK-5	PK-2	PK-12	K-12
Number Full Time Teachers	26.6	54.1	36.3	7,161.9	48,318
Pupil Teacher Ratio	13.0	14.4	15.1		
Population of Students Served					
African American	35.1	26.1	27.9	19.8	36.1
Asian	15.7	5.8	11.1	12.6	4.0
Latino	40.6	52.1	50.3	12.5	3.7
Native American	0.0	0.30	0.40	0.36	0.32
White	8.7	15.8	10.40	54.7	55.9

Table 1a. School Information Select Schools, School Districts and States, 1997-1998.

| | Montgomery Country, Maryland | | | | |
| | Schools | | | District | State |
	Martin	Morgan	MacLeod	Montgomery County	Maryland
Special Services					
Limited English	19.7	26.0	40.6	6.4	2.1
Title I	100	100	100	3.7	14.3
Free/Reduced Lunch	81.7	70.2	75.5	22.4	30.9
Special Education	13.3	9.3	5.5	11.8	12.5

SOURCES:

All Special Services information from MCPS (1998C). Montgomery County Public School Performance Report, 1998. Rockville, MD: Carver Educational Services Center.

School

MCPS (1997). *Schools at a glance.* Montgomery County Public Schools.

District

Race information based on NCES (1997). Common core of data agency universe, 1996-97.

State

NCES (1998c). *Common core of data state nonfiscal, 1997-98.*

Table 1b. School Information Select Schools, School Districts and States, 1997-1998.

	Philadelphia, Pennsylvania					
	Schools				*District*	*State*
	Parkland	Paine	Pine Crest	Phillips	Philadephia	Pennsylvania
Student Enrollment	386	394	1040	792	212,865	1,815,151
Grade Levels	K-4	K-5	K-8	K-4	K-12	K-12
Number Full Time Teachers	22	21	50	34	10,912.7	108,014
Pupil Teacher Ratio	17.5	18.8	20.8	23.3		
Population of Students Served						
African American	98.2	99.7	82.8	38.4	64	14.5
Asian	0.5	0.0	15.0	0.4	5	1.8
Latino	0.8	0.0	0.9	60.7	11	3.8
Native American	0.3	0.0	0.2	0.0	Not reported	.11
White	0.3	0.3	1.2	0.5	20	79.7

Table 1b. School Information Select Schools, School Districts and States, 1997-1998.

| | Philadelphia, Pennsylvania | | | | | |
| | Schools | | | | District | State |
	Parkland	Paine	Pine Crest	Phillips	Philadelphia	Pennsylvania
Special Services						
Limited English	0.0	0.0	6.4	4.8	4.0	Not reported
Title I	99.0	83.0	95.0	44.0	Not reported	Not reported
Free/Reduced Lunch	96.0	95.9	90.6	96.3	81.5	22
Special Education	0.7	1.5	2.8	2.7	11.0	Not reported

SOURCES:

School
Special services percentages based on 1995-1996 raw data provided by the district. All other statistics from NCES common core of data public elementary and secondary school universe, 1997-98.

District
Population of students served and special services statistics from "A citizen's guide to Philadelphia school budget, Philadelphia campaign for public education, 1997-98." All other statistics from NCES (1998a). Common core of data public agency universe, 1997-98.

State
NCES (1998c). *Common core of data state nonfiscal, 1997-98*, except Special Services Data.

Since 1988, Philadelphia schools with high proportions of at-risk students eligible for federal Title I aid began receiving their funding as schoolwide programs, which allows schools to use Title I funds for all children in the school. As of 1996-1997, all 169 of Philadelphia's Title I schools were schoolwide programs (Wong & Brown, 1998, p. 7-8).

In the MCPS the Title I program receives approximately 58% of its funds from the federal government, 21% from the state, and 21% from the county (MCPS, 1998b). As of the 1997-98 school year there were 58 schools in MCPS eligible to receive Title I funds. Of those 58, only four schools use the funds for schoolwide programs.[4]   Title I resources are allocated to eligible schools based on an educational load formula that "weights" the following four factors (MCPS, n.d.):

- The percentage of students approved for free and/or reduced price meals in each Title I eligible school;
- The actual number of free and/or reduced price lunch students enrolled in the school as of October 31;
- The percentage of students receiving ESOL services in each eligible school; and
- The mobility rate of the school's population.

As stated above, and shown in Table 1, the three schools in this study exceed the county and the state in percentage of students with limited English proficiency, receiving Title I, and receiving free/or reduced lunch. According to a Title I staff person in Montgomery County, schools are awarded two additional instructional assistant (I.A.) hours if they have an ESOL population higher than 11% and four additional hours if the population is higher than 20% (interview, Title I Specialist, MCPS, November 1997). Any school above the average mobility rate of 26.4% is awarded two additional I.A. hours.

Systemwide Level: Major Components of the Reform Initiatives

In addition to offering school districts more flexibility and authority in the use of Title I funds, the 1994 re-authorization of Title I legislation under IASA, "established the principle that Title I students will be taught to the same high standards as other children, and evaluates the performance of Title I schools and students using the same state standards and assessments that apply to all children" (Philadelphia, n.d. 3, p. 1). High standards for all children and "all children can learn" fall in line with the reform initiatives of both school districts. They are also the key assumptions of the systemic reform movement. These assumptions are supported by recent psychological theory and research that finds that all children engage in complex (higher-order) thinking tasks [and] *dumbing down* the material for the *disadvantaged* represents a clear denial of their opportunity to learn challenging material of the curriculum (O'Day & Smith, 1993, p. 264). Table 2 provides a comparison of the reform initiatives. The four components of *Success for Every Student* and seven of the ten components of the *Children Achieving Agenda* are included in this table.

We compare the reform initiatives of the two districts along four areas: standards, assessment, professional development, and partnership, with emphasis on reading and mathematics. We will analyze how the overlapping components of each plan affect teaching and learning for all students in the district and individual schools. We focus on the elementary grades.

Table 2. Major Components of the Two Reform Initiatives.

Name	*Success for Every Student* Plan Montgomery County	*Children Achieving Action* Plan Philadelphia
Adopted	January 6, 1992	February 6, 1995
Design	The plan provides broad strategies together with specific tasks for schools, central administrative offices and other departments, parents and communities. It identifies specific outcomes for student achievement among all racial/ethnic groups and provides a systemwide focus and direction. Furthermore, the plan provides an accountability element to ensure the full and successful completion of each responsibility.	The plan delineates the steps for four and one-half years (starting from 1995) to lead the city's public school children into the 21st century confident of the future. Its scope ranges from the new high standards our students must meet to compete in our global economy to the additional time our teachers will need to prepare students to meet those standards; and from the implementation of full-day kindergarten and smaller class sizes to the reorganization of the entire School District.

Name	*Success for Every Student Plan Montgomery County*	*Children Achieving Action Plan Philadelphia*
Belief that all students can and will achieve at high levels.[1]	**Ensure Success for Every Student** Provide the services and environment each student needs for intellectual challenge and social and emotional development. Each student will be able to communicate effectively, obtain and use information, solve problems, and engage in active, life-long learning. (Goal 1)	**Set high expectations for everyone.** The challenge we face is both inside and outside the schoolhouse door. It is about high expectation for us all. The first component of Children Achieving does not apply just to students. High Expectations calls on all of us to perform significantly better and differently than we have been performing. (Component 1)
Standards and Assessment	**Provide an Effective Instructional Program** Teach all students a curriculum that describes what they should know and be able to do, includes the many perspectives of a pluralistic society, and establishes learning standards. Instruction must include a variety of teaching strategies and technologies, actively involve students, and result in their mastery of learning objectives. (Goal 2)	**Set high expectations for everyone** (Component 1) **Design accurate performance indicators to hold everyone accountable for results.** At the end of the day, we can claim success only if students are successful in knowing and are able to do what they must to function effectively as good citizens and productive workers. We have failed if that does not occur. (Component 2)

Name	*Success for Every Student Plan Montgomery County*	*Children Achieving Action Plan Philadelphia*
Profess-ional Develop-ment	**Create a Positive Work Environment in a Self-Renewing Organization** Develop a climate in which staff effectiveness and creativity are encouraged, respected, valued and supported to promote productivity and ownership for student success. Provide efficient and effective support and staff development for the instructional program. (Goal 4)	**Provide intensive and sustained professional development to all staff.** Professional development must be intensive and sustained. It will involve observing good practice, practicing good practice, being coached in good practice, reflecting on good practice and repeating the process. It will emphasize building skill and knowledge teacher to teacher, being informed from time to time by both the opportunity to observe exemplary practice and to benefit from experts. (Component 4)
Partner-ships	**Strengthen Productive Partnerships for Education** Secure commitment of the entire community to maintain quality education in Montgomery County by building partnerships of families, community, business and staff that promote and support initiatives to help all children succeed. (Goal 3)	**Provide students with the community supports and services they need to succeed in school.** Community services and supports can make the difference between success and failure. Children who face the kinds of problems outside the school born of poverty will not achieve at high levels. Therefore it is imperative that initiatives be dramatically expanded to provide the necessary services and supports to reduce the impact of these major barriers to learning. (Component 6)

Name	Success for Every Student Plan Montgomery County	Children Achieving Action Plan Philadelphia
Partner-ships (cont.)		**Engage the public in shaping, understanding, supporting and participating i.. school reform.** Absent public understanding and support in both the neighborhoods and the boardrooms, we cannot provoke change in the first place nor sustain it into the future. (Component 8) **Make sure that all students are ready for school.** How civilized a country is can be determined by how it treats its young children. In partnership with other city and private agencies, we will approach the challenge in new and bold ways. Only by reducing the barriers that are built by inadequate support in the early years will we ensure a generation of young people who can maintain the economic and civic strengths that have made this nation great. (Component 5)

[1] Including those from low-income families, racial and language minorities, students with disabilities, and other populations.

SOURCES: School District of Montgomery County. (1994). *Success for Every Student* Plan: Vision and Goals, Outcomes, Strategies and Assessment. School District of Philadelphia. (1995). Action Design *Children Achieving*.

Standards - High Expectations

Philadelphia. The underlying premise of Philadelphia's *Children Achieving* plan is the standard "that all children can and will achieve at high levels." The school district has created content and performance standards that apply to all students in the district. The Philadelphia academic content standards and cross cutting competencies tell what students should know and be able to do in and across all the subject areas. They were approved by the Philadelphia Board of Education in September 1997. The standards tell what subject-specific knowledge and skills students should have, and benchmarks describe the general knowledge, skills, and concepts that students should know by the end of grades 4, 8, and 11 in order to achieve the broader standards. Cross-cutting competencies are common to all learning and should be integrated throughout all subject areas. They represent skills and awareness such as Communication, Technology, Problem-Solving, Citizenship, School-to-Career, and Multicultural Competence (School District of Philadelphia, 1999).

As guidelines for using the standards Philadelphia presented its Curriculum Frameworks to the teachers in February 1998. The frameworks (divided by grade level into a K-4 book, a 5-8 book, and a 9-12 book) explain what students should know and be able to do at each grade, give examples of what work the students can be doing to help them obtain these skills, include strategies for assessing the students' work, and name recommended resources and books, as well as instructional strategies, teachers can use in their classrooms (School District of Philadelphia, 1998).

At the elementary level, the Frameworks advise that reading should be taught to children at their instructional level (i.e., the level at which the child can best profit from instruction. This is the level at which the child can read aloud with 90-94% accuracy, and comprehend 75% of the information or story. This may be determined through retellings, running records, and Informal Reading Inventories). The framework cautions teachers and administrators against feeling pressured to instruct children with materials designated for a particular grade level before children acquire requisite skills and strategies to use them effectively. Other content area materials at grade level are expected to be part of each classroom's daily instruction through a shared reading experience (School District of Philadelphia, 1998).

Table 3. Percentage of Grade 4 Students Proficient on Reading and Mathematics Standardized Tests for Three Consecutive Years

	Reading			Mathematics		
	1996	1997	1998	1996	1997	1998
Montgomery County						
District	69%	69%	72%		56%	57%
Martin	30%	27%	49%		23%	53%
Morgan	57%	42%	55%		30%	44%
Philadelphia						
District	16%	19%	23%	10%	14%	16%
Parkland	8%	15%	34%	8%	18%	14%
Paine	5%	9%	14%	7%	7%	4%
Pine Crest	7%	6%	8%	4%	10%	9%
Phillips	11%	9%	15%	3%	7%	4%

SOURCE: Montgomery County Public Schools. (December 1997a). *Annual Report on the Systemwide Outcome Measures: Success for Every Student Plan.* School District of Philadelphia. (March 1999). Office of Accountability and Assessment.

Montgomery County: Based on district level Criterion-Referenced Test (CRT) Scores. The CRT measures how well elementary and middle school students are learning and applying specific information and skills taught in the county schools. The proficient score means that a child is progressing well through the curriculum at grade level.

Philadelphia: Based on District Stanford-9 Achievement (SAT-9) Test scores. The SAT-9 covers a student's knowledge of facts as well as the ability to use those facts. These scores are based on the total number of students tested and are thus slightly higher than the percentages reported by the district which are based on the number of students enrolled during the time of the test, including number of students not tested.

Note: The publisher of the SAT-9 made errors scoring the 1995-96 and 1996-97 results (very few errors [less than 20] were made in 1996-1997). Although these errors were fixed in the performance indexes for all schools, the disaggregated data for 1995-1996 was never re-run with the corrected SAT-9 results. The impact of these errors was to assign some students higher performance levels than they had in fact achieved on the SAT-9.

The mathematics frameworks map the specific concepts and skills embedded in benchmarks for every grade level and every course. These documents also include examples of student work for each grade level and course. Most of the performance tasks can be used to assess what students know and can do. Some are appropriate for use in group work and others are projects which may cover several class periods or even weeks. Many have been designed to involve more than one of the standards or cross-cutting competencies. Suggested instructional and assessment strategies, along with resources and best practices, are also presented to support teachers implementing the standards in their classrooms (1998).

Montgomery County. Montgomery County's *Success for Every Student* (SES) plan is three years older than Philadelphia's reform initiative, yet it is not as detailed. The underlying premise is similar to that in Philadelphia – all children can learn and schools are ethically responsible to teach all children. The 1992 plan provides broad strategies together with specific tasks for schools, central administrative offices and other departments, parents and communities. The tasks are designed to concentrate attention on the achievement of twelve specific outcome measures. The 1998 updated plan and draft material expands and redefines the strategic goals of the plan.

The updated plan provides ways to build synergy between continuous improvement and community collaboration. This plan presents an expansive perspective on the role of all students, staff, and community members in ensuring success for every student and places a high value on shared responsibility of staff and the community for student success (Montgomery County, 1998d). The plan provides a high level of flexibility while maintaining a sharp focus on outcomes and key results.

The MCPS Instructional Program in Reading/Language Arts and English was based on current research about language, language learning, and effective instruction, and addressed both content and process (MCPS, 1999b). The Instructional System in Mathematics (ISM) was used to provide teachers with: (1) a consistent description of learning outcomes, (2) tests to provide approximate starting points, (3) resources to support the individual instructional planning of teachers, (4) consistent assessment recommendations for judging student progress, and (5) reports to show student achievement in various formats for communication and planning purposes (MCPS, 1999a).

Assessment

Both school districts recognized the dangers of singular reliance on multiple choice and nationally-normed tests, and turned to criterion-referenced or performance-based assessments. These assessments measure how students fare against a standard. In addition, the needs of students of diverse language backgrounds were accommodated.

Philadelphia. In 1996, the Philadelphia school district discontinued the use of the California Test of Basic Skills (CTBS) in favor of the Stanford Achievement Test (SAT-9). The district also implemented a Spanish language test, the Spanish Language Aprenda. The SAT-9, which meshed well with the district emphasis on standards-driven instruction and performance assessment, retains the multiple-choice format but also includes "open-ended" questions. These questions require students to construct an answer that might involve writing or drawing a chart or graph, and typically require the student to analyze information, make inferences, and draw conclusions. The open-ended questions are graded according to a detailed scoring guide. A group of educators create a scoring guide that includes a working standard for determining degrees of proficiency in the skill being measured (School District of Philadelphia, 1997).

Philadelphia also has an incentive system based directly on the performance of students and schools. The Professional Responsibility Index sets targets every two years which will bring every school to high levels of achievement in one student generation (twelve years). A score of 95 is the twelve year target. Schools are not compared to other schools; rather, each school is compared against its own baseline performance over time. The plan provides penalties and rewards for schools depending on SAT-9 test scores, promotion rates, and attendance.

Montgomery County. The accountability component of the MCPS plan includes twelve outcomes for students that focus on Goals 1 and 2 of the SES plan: to ensure success for every student, and to provide an effective instructional program. As of June 1998, there were no outcomes that focused on Goals 3 and 4

(MCPS, 1998d, p. 5). As a method of measuring student profi-ciency and systemic evaluation the school district turned to criterion-referenced tests (CRTs), first administered in Spring 1994 in grades three through eight. In 1997, the math CRT was expanded to include an open-ended section. In addition, the standard for the multiple-choice section was raised in grades three, four, and five. These changes were expected to produce higher student achievement, provide greater prediction of future success, and allow for earlier intervention for students performing below standard (MCPS, 1997a). According to the MCPS Assessment booklet, the CRTs closely matched what is taught in the class-rooms and gave students different ways of showing what they knew. These tests also allowed students to demonstrate what they learned by solving "real life" problems.

The standard for individual student performance in MCPS was a score of 650 or above on the CRT. The standard for individual school performance was that 75% to 100% of eligible students taking the test met the individual student standard by 1999. The standard for school system performance was that 100% of the schools administering the tests had 75% to 100% of the eligible students meeting the individual student standard by 1999 (MCPS, 1997a).

Professional Development

Each district realizes that one cannot expect all students to achieve at high standards without providing teachers and other school staff with the training and tools they need to teach the standards. In Philadelphia the school district provides the resources equivalent, the cost of providing a substitute, of 20 days for all school-based teachers, administrators and staff, in support of the District's commitment to the capacity development of School District personnel. Schools have a network of people provided by the Cluster office who provide support in curriculum, instruction, and assessment. The network of people, the Teaching and Learning Network[5] (TLN), consists of the Teaching and Learning Coordinator, Teaching and Learning Facilitators and Equity Coordinator. There are after school and Saturday paid workshops about curriculum.

As part of the *Success for Every Student* reform four or five days are set aside for professional development in addition to the training and workshops that schools and teachers choose to participate in. Each school's improvement efforts include training based on the analysis of student achievement data disaggregated by gender and race, and other staff training needs (MCPS, 1994, p. 34).

Partnerships

The school districts of Philadelphia and Montgomery County have made great efforts to involve parents and the community in the schools. Some of the efforts include strategies that link students and families with needed health and social service supports, link schools with at least one community based organization, and recruit volunteers in the schools. Parents also must be involved in the writing of the school improvement plans.

Reform at the School and Classroom Levels

Philadelphia. Earlier studies of the implementation of the *Children Achieving* agenda showed evidence that the program's introduction was met with considerable confusion and resistance at the sub-district level and school level (Wong & Brown, 1998, p. 4). At the school level there were reports that the teachers and principals felt overloaded and while schools were expected to begin implementing many components of the new reform program simultaneously, surveys showed that in reality, schools only focused on starting one or two initiatives at a time, weaving them into existing programs (Wong & Brown, 1998, p. 4). At the classroom level, activities were shaped by strategies in place before *Children Achieving*; "the new reforms were simply added on top of earlier initiatives" (Wong & Sunderman, 1997, p. 8; also see Wong & Sunderman, 2000). In the second year of the Philadelphia initiative teachers, principals, Teaching and Learning Coordinators, and school staff reported that new curriculum and assessment priorities were beginning to be integrated into activities of professional development, planning sessions, lesson plans, instruction, assessment, and testing at the school and classroom level (Wong & Brown, p. 18).

When we visited the schools during the third year of the reform and asked how schools applied state- and district-wide standards we were informed that the Curriculum Frameworks had recently been introduced to the teachers. One teacher from the Paine school mentioned the Frameworks as the curriculum she used with students. She said that "there is flexibility in the use of the curriculum . . . . It is fabulous. I use a lot of the suggestions" (interview, third grade teacher, Paine, February 1998). Another teacher at that same school said that the standards are the same for all students. "There is no lower benchmark" (interview, fifth grade teacher, Paine, February 1998). In fact there is a reminder in the *Children Achieving* school improvement plan that "whatever instructional strategies and assessments that are developed for regular education students should be reflected through adapted instruction and assessments for special education students." Sections of each school improvement plan are devoted to strategies for implementing standards-driven instruction/assessment in reading/language arts and mathematics and other components of the reform initiative.

Principals at Parkland and Phillips stated that the overall goal for their school was to have all children reading on grade level. This was also an evident goal at Paine as seen through interviews and classroom observations. The schools varied on the strategies used to implement this goal. Paine used "story mapping, story retelling (one of the strategies of the Curriculum Frameworks), Venn diagrams (graphic organizers), meta-cognition strategies, word maps, open-ended questions, vocabulary awareness, performance tasks and writing journals" (interview, Reading Resource teacher, Paine, February 1998) to teach children. The schools integrate reading in all subject areas. Parkland uses the Houghton-Mifflin Program to incorporate writing, math, science and social studies in every lesson. A schoolwide journal writing program was added to the program during the 1997-98 school year (Parkland's School Improvement Plan, 1997-98). Thematic units are used to integrate reading in all subject areas at Phillips, a predominantly Latino school. An example of some of these strategies and other strategies used at the schools are seen at Phillips during observation of a third grade reading lesson.

> Students continue reading "Sing Little Sack" !Canto Saquito!. The teacher reviews the skill of predicting. She asks the class what is predicting. A student responds correctly. The task for the day is story retelling and sequencing. Teacher asks students where the story takes place. A student responds - Puerto Rico. Teacher asks students to find Puerto Rico on the map that was handed out earlier [integration of reading with social studies]. She asks what

bodies of waters are north and south of Puerto Rico. Two students respond correctly. The teacher writes on the board as different students give her the sequence of events in the story. After they are finished there are eight sentences on the board which the teacher asks students to read. Books are handed out and they begin reading where they left off in the story. Since part of the story is in Spanish, the Spanish speaking students read those parts of the story. Students raise their hands and are called on to read. The teacher walks around the room to see that other students are following along with the reader. They reach a stopping point in the story and the teacher asks them to write down what they predict will happen next (third grade classroom observation, Phillips, February 1998).

The focus area for Pine Crest during the 1997-98 school year was mathematics based on their SAT-9 scores. Grades Two through Eight use the Jumping Levels as an ongoing program for assessment and for basic fact practice (Pine Crest's School Improvement Plan, 1997-98/99). Paine's math program for grades one through five, including Special Education, addresses the math standards and emphasizes problem solving with a problem of the day. Problem solving activities, performance-based assessments, and the extensive use of manipulatives are common strategies throughout all four schools. The principal at Paine reported that the main thrust for the year was performance-based standards. She said that "the school's vision is tied into our performance index. We had two years to improve performance by 10% in SAT-9, promotion, and attendance. We were able to reach it in one year" (interview, principal, Paine, February 1998). Improving critical thinking skills seems to be a common thread for all schools. All schools use small group instruction, particularly for students with special needs, and cooperative learning to assist in reading and mathematics.

During 1997-98 there was extensive staff development regarding the Standards, Curriculum Frameworks and the Comprehensive Support Process. The Comprehensive Support Process was a means of "creating a bridge of support services that meet the needs of all students in the least restrictive environment" (School District of Philadelphia, n.d. 1). The principal at Parkland described professional development as rich at her school, commenting that, "I encourage teachers to take observation days to visit other schools and teachers who are doing innovative things in their classrooms" (Interview, principal, Parkland, February, 1998). Teachers and other staff also participated in training geared toward the reading and mathematics strategies mentioned earlier.

Professional development provided by the Teaching and Learning Network (TLN) trained teachers to use the Curriculum Frameworks and to set up small learning communities. The TLN coordinator explained that professional development included "direct classroom support: workshops at the school and cluster level, [and training in ways to] facilitate meetings within schools [and] grade groups" (interview, Teaching and Learning Coordinator, Phillips, February, 1998). The TLN Coordinators worked with schools to determine the type of professional development needed for the year. Many teachers and principals mentioned that the training provided by TLN was key for that year.

In Philadelphia, the formation of small learning communities (SLCs) was an important strategy of the *Children Achieving* agenda. These learning communities served 200 to 500 students, thus a school could have had more than one SLC. These communities grouped students heterogeneously, and teachers were committed to enabling all students to achieve rigorous standards. The SLCs were accountable for student outcomes and had decision-making authority commensurate with that responsibility (School District of Philadelphia, 1995). Most SLCs formed around a particular theme, such as cultural diversity or technology.

Each of the schools we visited had two SLCs, and these were frequently mentioned as one of the most positive aspects of the *Children Achieving* agenda. Several teachers reported that SLCs gave them more time to plan with other teachers and to share instructional strategies, time that was not specifically organized for that purpose before (Wong & Brown, 1998, p. 22). However, some teachers and principals expressed frustration at the difficulty of regrouping hundreds of students, rearranging teaching schedules, and re-coordinating instruction time (Wong & Brown, p. 23)

An increase in parental involvement was needed in each of the schools. The job of the Home and Schooling Coordinator (a position funded by Title I) was to work with parents. During the school year Paine was preparing a workshop for parents to help their children. One goal was to plan more effective workshops for parents that addressed the standards, performance assessments, and preparation for the SAT-9 (Parkland's School Improvement Plan, 1997-98). All schools had volunteers to listen to the students read. These volunteers included parents and grandparents, Community Assistants, and volunteers from Americorp.

Montgomery County. Schools developed their own tasks and objectives for achieving the system goals in the form of the *Success for Every Student* (SES) School Improvement Plan. The plan consisted of reading/language arts, mathematics, and pupil service area objectives. In MCPS, when asked about the school's goals, each teacher and principal interviewed stated several aspects of the *Success for Every Student* plan and their local school plan. However, staff at Morgan additionally stated that their focus for the 1997-98 school year was writing across the curriculum. This focus was repeated in interviews and witnessed in classroom observations at the school, as detailed below.

- In the math class, the students used blocks and mats for regrouping and subtraction and had the students record each step.
- The principal reported examples of seeing students working with manipulatives and writing down what they were doing.
- Students used graphic organizers to complete a research project on animals. The lesson integrated reading, writing and social studies.

Staff at Martin and Morgan identified program differentiation and high expectations under the "all children can learn" theme as positive aspects of the SES plan. On the negative side, one teacher at Morgan complained that differentiation resulted in more work; "You cannot only plan for two or three subjects. You're planning for two or three levels" (interview, fifth grade teacher, Morgan, March, 1998). Also, there was the complaint at both schools of not having enough time to implement the objectives. "If you are in a meeting every week, when do you have the time to implement? They ask for certain proof before we are able to show them" (interview, principal, Morgan, March, 1998).

Teachers at Martin felt pressured by the testing. One teacher commented that the vision of the school was passing the state tests. When the research staff visited this teacher's math class in March, the teacher had discontinued normal lesson planning and was focusing on preparing the students for the Maryland State Performance Assessments and CRTs which would take place in May. Students spent the entire class taking Instructional System in Math (I.S.M.) tests which they are required to pass before going on to another topic/level in math. Students are responsible for mastering a certain number of objectives per marking period. I.S.M. testing goes on every week.

Each school improvement plan listed various strategies for implementing the stated objectives and goals of the reform, all of which involved increasing CRT achievement over the next two years by 10 points each year. There was little variation among the three schools regarding strategies for teaching reading: reading incentives programs, Writer's Workshop, Daily Drop Everything and Read (DEAR) and Read Aloud Times, writing to inform and persuade, interpreting expository discourse from various sources, listening stations, and the utilization of computers to complete research reports.

There were variations in student grouping in math classes, however. At Martin, students were regrouped for math and reading/language arts by ability. At MacLeod, students were heterogeneously grouped. According to an interview with the Magnet Coordinator at MacLeod, "There is heterogeneous grouping in the first grade because that is good for the kids. [I]t is irreparable the damage to kids that homogenous grouping can do. Kids need that spark in the classroom. [The school] has done research on this."

The SES plan at Morgan and MacLeod stated in detail the strategies to be used in mathematics instruction. These strategies included the use of prompts, rubrics, manipulatives, and 'real life' problems. Although not stated in their SES plan, some of these strategies were also used at Martin.

When asked about typical instructional strategies, the common thread across schools was the use of small groups. This practice, however, was observed more frequently at Morgan and MacLeod, than at Martin. During the reading lesson at Morgan, instructional assistants worked with a small group of students who needed additional help, while the teacher worked with the rest of the class. According to those interviewed, other strategies used with students needing extra assistance were direct instruction, shared reading, readjustment of the lesson, individual instruction, repetition, and extra time.

It was common at Morgan to have two reading groups within the same class. In MacLeod, students often worked in centers. In one class the students broke up into reading centers - Read the room, Silent read, Poetry corner, and Write own story. There were groups of five or six students at each center. The teacher and instructional assistant both worked with small groups. Only in one classroom in Martin was there observed differentiation in the instructional strategies used in the classroom. A third grade teacher pulled three students to listen to a tape of the story that the rest of the class was reading. They were instructed to read along with the tape. For the most part, all students were working on the same assignment in Martin.

In MCPS it was apparent at each school that the schoolwide use of the instructional assistants (IAs) was the greatest bene-fit/resource. According to the principal at Morgan,

prior to the [schoolwide program] we had to restrict the use of the Title I instructional assistants. Now we can do it from kindergarten through fifth grade and that's very helpful because children leaving fourth grade do not all of the sudden not need the extra coaching or the extra involvement of the Title I aide (interview, princi-pal, Morgan, November, 1997).

The responsibilities of IAs are to work directly with the students and not to be an aide to the teacher. Each teacher observed had an IA working in the classroom at some point during the reading and mathematics lessons that were observed.

Morgan used the IAs more effectively. At Morgan IAs would work with a small group while the teacher worked with the remaining class. At Martin the IAs were mostly used to grade test papers. Despite the increased presence of IAs in the classrooms, "teachers complain that [the IAs are always being taken] out for meetings and training and kids are missing time with assistants" (interview, Title I administrator, Morgan, November, 1997). Similar complaints were made by teachers at Morgan; during one of the school visits the IAs were called out of the classrooms for a meeting with the principal that lasted approximately half an hour. The schools in Philadelphia also have classroom and supportive assistants, but their presence was not as prominent in the classrooms that were visited in MCPS.

There is a great deal of professional development on teaching and assessment strategies at each school. As part of the *Success for*

Every Student reform, "certain days are designated for schools to look at test data and to analyze it and develop a plan to address areas that need to be reinforced/improved" (interview, Title I administrator, Morgan, November, 1997).

As in Philadelphia, parental involvement in MCPS is not as great as principals and teachers would like. "Parents are involved typically when students perform or are chaperones on field trips" (interview, principal, Martin, March, 1998). Title I provides meetings by grade level to inform parents about what they can do to help their children be successful in school. Our staff attended two of these sessions in November. Literature and handouts are provided and a translator, if necessary. MacLeod also has a school leadership team that consists of, in addition to the principal, teachers and other staff, a parent coordinator and a couple of parents. The team meets monthly.

Morgan is involved with different county agencies, social services, protective services, child welfare services, that deliver health services as well as ethnic support groups such as Casa de Maryland, NAACP, and an African American Sorority. In addition, "senior citizens that belong to an intergeneration bridges group come in once or twice a week and work with children who are non-English speaking and help them in a social context, mentor them" (interview, principal, Morgan, November, 1997).

To summarize, the schoolwide programs in the four schools in Philadelphia and three schools in Montgomery County appear to be moving toward "systemic" reform. Overall, our case studies of Title I schoolwide programs in the two districts suggest that the schools are making efforts to move toward systemic improvements:

- Standards are in place – schools and teachers have incorporated them into the schools' goals and take them seriously.
- Professional development is found in the schools that we visited.
- There is flexibility at the school and classroom levels to enable experiments and innovation in the instructional strategies.

What the Test Scores Say

Although our study has focused on the implementation of reforms, we also consider the performance at the district and school levels disaggregated by race/ethnic level. Table 3 illustrates the percentage of students meeting the district standard for proficiency in reading and mathematics at the district and school levels for grade four for Spring 1996, 1997 and 1998. Information for MacLeod is not provided because it is a kindergarten through second grade school. Table 4 shows the same information disaggregated by race/ethnicity. These percentages are based on the number of students who were tested.

At the district level, reform seemed to have improved student achievement over the three year period that we analyzed. Based on each districts' assessment standards, a higher percentage of fourth graders in MCPS attained proficiency than their counterparts in Philadelphia. Approximately 70% of MCPS' fourth graders were proficient in reading during the three years, as opposed to only 16% of the fourth graders in Spring 1996, 19% in Spring 1997 and 23% in Spring 1998 in Philadelphia. In mathematics the differences are not as dramatic, however, over 55% of students in MCPS were proficient compared to 10% in Spring1996, 14.2% in Spring 1997, and 16.1% in Spring 1998. However, if we consider the percentages for the students with partial proficiency in reading and mathematics (basic level) in Philadelphia, the percentages for MCPS and Philadelphia are comparable.

Our case study schools suggest uneven student progress by subject areas during the three years. At the school level there is not much difference between the percentages for the four schools in Philadelphia and the overall school district percentages. The percentages are equally low for each school. In all cases, except at Parkland in Spring 1998, the percentages of students proficient in reading and math at each school were lower than the district percentages. In fact, Spring 1998 witnessed a decrease in the proficiency percentages from the previous year. In the two schools in MCPS the overall percentages in most cases are less than half the percentages for reading for the whole school district for the corresponding school year. The percentages in Morgan are higher than Martin.[7] In math the percentages for the schools are lower but it is important to note that at Martin the percentage of students proficient in math almost doubled from Spring 1997 to Spring 1998 and at Morgan the percentages increased by more than a third.

Looking at the percentages for the Montgomery County district and schools disaggregated by race/ethnic group (Table 4), we see a large gap between white and African American and Latino percentages. In most cases, the District-wide gap is smaller than at the individual schools, but it is still large and remains relatively the same for the three years. The differences are between 34 and 39 percentage points in reading and 33 and 44 percentage points in math. For Asian American students the differences are relatively small. Additionally, there is not much difference in the gap between the percentages for African American fourth graders and white fourth graders and the gap between Latino and white students. At Martin the gap is much greater between the white and African American students than the white and Latino and white and Asian American students, with the gap between Asian American and white students being the smallest. At Morgan the reverse is true, the gap between Latino and white students is greater than the gap between African American and white students. This can possibly be explained by the fact that almost 50% of Morgan's student population is Latino as opposed to 40% of Martin's population.

The disaggregated percentages for students who scored proficient or above at the four schools in Philadelphia do not tell us anything more substantial than the percentages for the schools overall, since these schools are predominately African American or predominately Latino and African American. It is important to note that Philadelphia has increased the number of students taking the tests. "Across all three subjects [science is the other subject tested], 93.5% of fourth graders participated in Spring 1998. This is an increase of 9.0 points from 1995-96, when 84.5% took the test" (School District of Philadelphia, n.d. 2, p.3).

Conclusion

This research provides only a snapshot of the complex reform initiatives in Title I schoolwide programs in Montgomery County and Philadelphia. Despite their many differences, the two districts seem to be fairly similar in their experiences in systemic improvements. They use similar standards, similar types of assessments, and similar instructional strategies. We see that the goals and strategies of the reforms are not just words that one finds written in a lengthy plan or that only the administration has read, but are actually being implemented in the schools and classrooms. Also, each district does not seem to be wedded to their plans and allows for flexibility in the way schools and teachers implement the reforms. In short, efforts are being made toward "systemic reform" in the Title I schoolwide programs that we studied.

Interestingly, our study suggests promising strategies in Title I schoolwide programs. Parkland in Philadelphia, in particular, showed significant academic improvement during the three years of our study. It implemented extensive professional development programs, involved parents and grandparents to participate in a children's literacy initiative, and maintained a small enrollment. In MCPS, Morgan seemed to improve its math test performance because they practiced ISM on a weekly basis with the support of instructional assistants.

Progress made in the three-year trend notwithstanding, the proficiency levels present a less than positive picture of achievement in both school districts. Given the relative newness of the reforms in the school districts, it would not be realistic to expect the goal of providing academic success for all students to be accomplished in such a short time frame. Students must have had the opportunity to learn well the material on the assessment (O'Day & Smith, 1993, p. 286). When can we say enough time has passed? How do we know that teachers are teaching the material? The latter question would require further research at the classroom level (see Wong, et al. 1999).

Nonetheless, allowing for the newness of the tests does not address the issue of why certain students are performing better than others on the same test. The gap between the white students and most minority students still persists in Montgomery County, remaining relatively the same in most cases and in some cases widening from one year to the next for some ethnic and racial groups. It is important to note that although MCPS saw *Success for Every Student* as a plan that would allow it to address minority achievement without provoking opposition from the larger population, there has been criticism that the goals are far too general without specific strategies for improving performance goals for minority students (Jones & Hill, 1997, p. 18). Additionally, O'Day and Smith (1993) cautioned that the widening of the measured gap would be exacerbated if the achievement measures place a greater emphasis on higher-order skills and content to which large numbers of poor students have not been given access (p. 260). These are the type of assessments used in MCPS and Philadelphia. These gaps clearly call for greater districtwide efforts to ensure that minority students have access to quality instruction.

Notes

1. To insure confidentiality pseudonyms have been used for all schools in the two districts.
2. The selection process for the schools in Montgomery County was different from the process for Philadelphia. Montgomery County only has four schools that use Title I funds schoolwide. Three of those schools were used in this study.
3. For the purpose of this discussion we will focus only on public school enrollment
4. In schools with schoolwide programs, all students enrolled are counted as Title I participates, as indicated in Table 1.
5. From November 1997 interview with Title I Specialist in MCPS.
6. The Teaching and Learning Network is designed to provide cluster support to teachers for improving instructional strategies and to assist learning communities and schools to develop instructional programs. The Network includes a coordinator and six to eight facilitators for each cluster. The Network is structured to train selected teachers and principals from each school, who then provide turn-around training in the schools. It also provides staff development on such things as the development of small learning communities, team building, and the implementation of standards.
7. In mid-May of 1998 it came down from the superintendent's office that Martin and MacLeod, which is the feeder school (grades pre K - 2) for Martin will share one administrator and each school will have an assistant principal. The current principal at MacLeod is the administrator. The decision was based on 1996-97 county and state test scores on which Martin did very poorly. Over the last four months the community was very vocal and active in wanting a change. This became effective as of Fall

1998. During the 1996-97 school year on which this decision was based grade 3 was at MacLeod.

References

Jones, C. and Hill, C. (1997). *Strategies and tactics in subsystem protection: The politics of education reform in Montgomery County, Maryland.* University of Maryland College Park, unpublished paper.

Montgomery County Public Schools. (1994). *Success for every student plan: Vision and goals, outcomes, strategies and assessments.* Montgomery County Public Schools, Maryland.

Montgomery County Public Schools. (1997). Schools at a glance, 1997-98. Montgomery County Public Schools, Maryland.

Montgomery County Public Schools. (1998a). *Annual report on the systemwide outcome measures: Success for every student plan.* Montgomery County Public Schools, Maryland.

Montgomery County Public Schools. (1998b). *Education and quality investment: Montgomery County Public Schools Title I handbook for teachers and instructional assistants.*

Montgomery County Public Schools. (1998c). Montgomery County school performance report, 1998. Rockville, MD: Carver Educational Services Center.

Montgomery County Public Schools. (1998d). *Success for every student plan: A strategic plan for the MCPS future.* Montgomery County Public Schools, Maryland.

Montgomery County Public Schools. (1999a). General overview of ISM. Montgomery County, Maryland: Author. Retrieved March 24, 1999 from World Wide Web: http://www.mcps.md.us/schools/stonegates/ism.

Montgomery County Public Schools. (1999b). Reading/ Language Arts & English. Montgomery County, Maryland: Author. Retrieved March 24, 1999 from World Wide Web: http://www.mcps.md.us/curriculum/english.

Montgomery County Public Schools (n.d.). Title I handbook for teachers and instructional assistants. Montgomery County, Maryland.

National Center for Education Statistics. (1997). Common core of data agency universe, 1996-97. Washington, D. C.: Author. Retrieved [March 11, 1999] from the Common Core of

Data database on the World Wide Web: http://nces.ed.gov/ccd/pubagency.html.

National Center for Education Statistics. (1998a). Common core of data agency universe, 1997-98. Washington, D. C.: Author. Retrieved [March 24, 2000] from the Common Core of Data database on the World Wide Web: http://nces.ed.gov/ccd/pubagency.html.

National Center for Education Statistics. (1998b). Common core of data public elementary and secondary school universe, 1997-98. Washington, D. C.: Author. Retrieved [March 30, 2000] from the Common Core of Data database on the World Wide Web: http://nces.ed.gov/ccd/pubschuniv.html.

National Center for Education Statistics. (1998c). Common core of data state nonfiscal, 1997-98. Washington, D. C.: Author. Retrieved [March 24,2000] from the Common Core of Data database on the World Wide Web: http://nces.ed.gov/ccd/stNfis.html.

National Center for Education Statistics. (1999). Characteristics of the 100 largest public elementary and secondary school districts in the United States: 1997-98. Washington, D. C.: Author. Retrieved March 24, 2000 from World Wide Web: http://nces.ed.gov/pubsearch/pubsinfo.asp?pubid=1999318.

O'Day, J. and Smith, M. (1993). Systemic reform and educational opportunity. In S. Fuhrman (ed.) *Designing coherent educational policy: Improving the system.* San Francisco: Jossey-Bass.

School District of Philadelphia. (1995). *Children achieving action design.* Philadelphia, PA.

School District of Philadelphia. (1997). There's a new test in town. *Philadelphia Public School Notebook,* 4(2), 5.

School District of Philadelphia. (1998). *Standards-driven instruction - school district of Philadelphia curriculum framework.* Philadelphia, PA: Author. Retrieved October 1998 from World Wide Web: http://www.philsch.k12.pa.us/offices/ curriculum/frameworks.

School District of Philadelphia. (1999). *Standards-driven instruction - school district of Philadelphia curriculum framework.* Philadelphia, PA: Author. Retrieved October 1998 from World Wide Web: http://www.philsch.k12.pa.us/offices/ curriculum/frameworks/standriv.

School District of Philadelphia. (n.d 1). *Implementing the comprehensive support process: An overview.* School District of Philadelphia, PA.

School District of Philadelphia. (n.d 2). *Sat-9 results: Philadelphia's achievement results.* School District of Philadelphia, PA.

School District of Philadelphia. (n.d 3). *Title I informational tickler file: An implementation guide for the Children Achieving educational plan and Title I initiatives.* Philadelphia, PA. Office of Standards, Equity, and Student Services, Title I Schoolwide Projects. School District of Philadelphia, PA.

U. S. Census Bureau. (1996, July). Model-based income and poverty estimates for Montgomery County, Maryland in 1995. Washington, D. C.: Author. Retrieved November 30, 1999 from World Wide Web: http:// www.census.gov/hhs/www/saipe/estimate/cty/cty/cty24031.htm.

U. S. Census Bureau. (1996, July). Model-based income and poverty estimates for Philadelphia, Pennsylvania in 1995. Washington, D. C.: Author. Retrieved November 30, 1999 from World Wide Web: http:// www.census.gov/hhs/www/saipe/estimate/cty/cty/cty42101.htm.

Wang, M.C. and Wong, K. (1997) *Implementing School Reform.* Center for Research in Human Development and Education, Temple University: Philadelphia.

Wong, K., Anagnostopoulos, D., Rutledge, S., Lynn, L., and Dreeben, R. (1999) *Implementation of an Educationai Accountability Agenda: Integrated Governance in the Chicago Public Schools Enters its Fourth Year.* Department of Education and the Harris Graduate School of Public Policy Studies, University of Chicago: Chicago.

Wong, K. and Brown, J. (1998) *The implementation of two reform programs in Philadelphia: Lessons learned from Children Achieving and Title I schoolwide strategies,* University of Chicago, unpublished paper.

Wong, K. and Sunderman, G. (1997) The Effects of Reform on Title I Schoolwide Programs in Philadelphia, University of Chicago, unpublished paper.

Wong, K. and Sunderman, G. (2000) Implementing District-wide Reform in Schools with Title I Schoolwide Programs: The first two years of Children Achieving in Philadelphia. *Journal of Education for Students Placed At Risk,* 5-4.

Wong, K. and Wang, M.C., eds. (1994) *Rethinking Policy for At-Risk Students*. Berkeley, CA: McCutchan Publishing Corporation.

CHAPTER 6

TIMBER MOUNTAIN BREAKDOWN: HOW A FUZZY VISION DERAILED ONE SCHOOL'S REFORM EFFORT

Patricia E. Ceperley

Introduction

This is the story of an unsuccessful attempt by a high-poverty, low-achieving rural school to implement a schoolwide approach to school improvement. While the terms "high poverty" and "low achieving" typically call forth images of students in urban areas, these terms also characterize many rural schools. In addition, high-poverty, low-achieving rural schools often have less capacity than urban schools to change to meet newly established state mandated content and performance standards (Stapleton, 1998).

The Improving America's Schools Act (IASA) of 1994 championed the belief that all children can achieve when held to high standards and reflected effective schools research which suggests the school is the appropriate unit of improvement (Wong & Meyer, 1998). IASA permitted schools to develop schoolwide programs using various streams of federal funds, including Title I funds, in new and creative ways to meet the needs of all students in the school. This innovative approach had the potential for increasing the capacity of rural schools to meet the needs of their students.

National evaluations suggest that once schools adopt a schoolwide approach, they encounter implementation difficulties. Further, statistical analyses of test data from several cities and states show that some schools are significantly more effective than others at improving the academic performance of students from low-income families (Wang, Wong, & Kim, 1999). Standardized test scores at effective schools are higher than expected when social and demographic characteristics of the schools are controlled, and standardized test scores for less-effective schools are lower than expected.

The schoolwide program at Timber Mountain Elementary was studied as part of a larger research project that included four rural schools. The study is important because while several previous studies had examined implementation of schoolwide programs in urban areas, information about rural schoolwide programs was scant. The purpose of the current study was to identify the programmatic and organizational characteristics of schoolwide programs—specific components that might be related to the effectiveness of the schools (Ceperley, 1999).

Timber Mountain Elementary School

Data were collected using interview protocols developed collaboratively by representatives of five regional education laboratories. Researchers observed third, fourth, and fifth grade English/language arts and mathematics lessons, and interviewed six third, fourth, and fifth grade teachers, ten parents, the principal, and the Title I coordinator. District documents were also analyzed.

Timber Mountain Elementary School met these three criteria. First, researchers established that Timber Mountain Elementary was located in a rural area—serving an area with fewer than 2,500 inhabitants or a zip code defined as rural by the U.S. Bureau of the Census—according to the Johnson codes. Johnson codes classify school locales as one of seven types, ranging from "large city" to "rural" (Burczyk, 1998).

Second, the school's performance was less effective than expected (Yancey, Breeding, & Freely, 1998). Virginia Department of Education (VDE) staff provided data on the pass rate on the Iowa Test of Basic Skills (ITBS), the proportion of students eligible for free or reduced-price lunches, attendance rate, and ethnicity of students for every public school in the Commonwealth. Staff at the Laboratory for School Success (LSS)—the lead regional educational laboratory for the study of Title I

Schoolwide implementation—analyzed the data and identified Timber Mountain Elementary as a less-effective school.

Third, according to a list provided by the Virginia Department of Education, Timber Mountain Elementary had planned and implemented a Title I schoolwide program. The school was in its second year of implementation.

Timber Mountain Elementary is located in central Virginia, where the economy depends primarily on agriculture. Of the approximately 300 students in kindergarten through fifth grades, most were at risk for early school failure. As seen in Table 1, 75% qualify for free or reduced-price lunch; more than 60% are African American; and the attendance rate for 1991-92 through 1996-97 was 82%. From 1991 through 1997, Timber Mountain Elementary students performed below expectations. More than 13% fewer students passed the Iowa Test of Basic Skills than were expected to, according to a statistical analysis that predicted the percentage of passing scores while controlling for ethnicity, SES, and average daily attendance.

Table 1. Characteristics of Timber Mountain Elementary School

Timber Mountain Elementary	Characteristics
Johnson Code Classification	Rural
Attendance Rate	82%
Percent Low-SES	80%
African American Population	62.3%
Predicted Pass Rate on ITBS	38.9
Observed Pass Rate on ITBS	25.5
Gap Between Predicted and Observed ITBS Scores	-13.4
Year of School-wide Program Implementation	2

Findings

The State Context

Although Virginia does not appropriate funds to match federal Title I funds, the General Assembly has established a long-term goal of reducing pupil-teacher ratios and class sizes for grades kindergarten through third in those schools in the Commonwealth with high or moderate concentrations of at-risk students. Pupil-teacher ratios and class sizes for schools volunteering to participate in this program are set in the annual budget for public education. In addition, the state provides funds in its annual budget that the Virginia Department of Education can allocate in the form of grants to schools or other community agencies that want to operate programs for four-year-olds and kindergarten age children that are not otherwise served.

Documents collected during the study showed that during the past decade, Virginia had implemented policies that incorporated the major components of systemic education reform needed to guide local school improvement. These components included content standards, student assessments, and accreditation standards.

Content standards. Rigorous grade-by-grade content standards, called the Virginia Standards of Learning (SOL), for kindergarten through twelfth grade in English/language arts, mathematics, science, and history/social science, were adopted by the state board of education in 1995 and are part of the state education code. Within these statutory constraints, Virginia schools are free to design their own curricula to achieve the standards. Schools are urged to institute programs that identify students at risk of failure and that prevent students from dropping out. Local boards are required to "revise, extend, and adopt" a 6-year improvement plan that is developed in collaboration with school staff and community members, and each school must prepare a biennial plan that is consistent with the board's six-year plan.

Student assessments. A new Standards of Learning (SOL) assessment system, which was designed specifically to monitor student performance relative to the new standards, was adopted and pilot tested in the spring of 1997. Results were first made public in 1998.

Accreditation standards. In 1997, the state board of education approved new school accreditation standards that call for increased school accountability and higher graduation requirements. Accreditation standards for schools will be applied in 2006-07. For a school to become fully accredited, 70% of its students must pass SOL tests at the end of third, fifth, and eighth grades, and at the end of high school courses (third grade history and science require only a 50% pass rate).

The District Context

Timber Mountain Elementary is one of three primary schools (pre-kindergarten though third grade) in the district, but it is the only one that also houses fourth and fifth grades. All three primary schools had Title I schoolwide programs, but Timber Mountain Elementary was selected for study because the study design specified a focus on grades three through five. The district's director of federal programs was coordinator of Title I programs as well as Title II, Title VI, special education, early childhood, and federal lunch and breakfast programs. She indicated that the district decided to adopt a schoolwide approach because of the flexibility it offered the district and schools for using federal funding streams.

According to district reports, the district's Title I allocation was about $383,000, or nearly $640 per low-income pupil in eligible schools. The district office set aside about $51,000 for administration, and the remainder was allocated to the three primary schools in the district. Timber Mountain Elementary received Title I funds totaling nearly $138,000. According to the district Title I coordinator, Title I funds to the district had decreased by $50,000 to $150,000 over the past few years. So, the district decided to narrow the focus of the Title I program from students in grades K-6 to those in K-3.

In an effort to bolster the learning of at-risk students, district officials decided to maintain existing programs for four-year-olds in each of the primary schools. They used Title I funds to support the program in Timber Mountain Elementary and state funds to support the programs in the other two schools.

The Title I coordinator indicated that Title I funds were used by the district in combination with other federal, state, and local funds for implementing schoolwide programs to "upgrade the entire educational program in eligible schools." In eligible elementary schools, Title I monies were used to fully or partially fund staffing to allow the following programs to continue:

- Developmental Learning Center,
- Project F.O.U.R.—Fostering Our Unique Resources—a model school-based early childhood program for at-risk four-year-olds,
- Mobile Learning Center to provide developmentally appropriate instructional experiences for students, offer educational opportunities and literacy/social support during visits to school and home sites, and extend adult training opportunities such as preparation for taking the GED Test, and
- Mentor and Peer-Helper Program for secondary school students.

Title I Schoolwide Program At Timber Mountain Elementary

Timber Mountain Elementary planned its Title I schoolwide program during the 1995-96 school year and began implementation of the program in 1996-97. The Timber Mountain schoolwide plan included these six goals:

- Employ a highly qualified staff.
- Provide professional development training.
- Increase parent involvement.
- Provide opportunities for all students to meet state standards.
- Provide extended learning opportunities for students with learning difficulties.
- Continue the pre-school program.

Teachers, parents, the principal, and the Title I coordinator were questioned about these six goals during interviews. Although teachers who were interviewed were aware of the Title I program and how it worked at the school, neither the teachers nor the parents indicated an awareness of the planning process for the schoolwide program.

Qualified Staff

Although the schoolwide plan for Timber Mountain established as a goal "employing a highly qualified staff," the teachers appeared to have a wide range of experience and training. The responses of the six teachers who were asked about the degrees and areas of certification they held are shown in Table 2. District documents stated that 67% of the teachers at Timber Mountain had master's degrees or above. In addition, the Title I teacher was a reading specialist.

Table 2. Teacher Qualifications

	Degree	**Certification**	**Years of Experience**
Teacher A	Master	Reading	12
Teacher B	Bachelor	Education (Grades 4-8)	8
Teacher C	Bachelor	Elementary (Grades 1-7)	27
Teacher D	Bachelor	Education (Grades K-8)	7
Teacher E	Bachelor	Elementary (Grades K-6)	1
Teacher F	Bachelor	Elementary (Grades K-7)	21

Professional Development

Although providing professional development was a component of the schoolwide plan, the school did not appear to have a schoolwide approach to professional development. There were many competing demands for staff development time at Timber Mountain Elementary. One teacher said,

> We had a lot of in-service this year—developing benchmarks, meeting with other grade-level teachers, and developing new report cards, but I don't see that as in-service.

Another teacher indicated that there had been an increase in professional development, workshops, and classes with an emphasis on at-risk students over the past four to five years.

Several teachers commented that most of the professional development had been about the SOLs. Computer technology had been added to the SOLs and teachers took computer classes. They also participated in demonstrations by several companies selling software. Teachers said staff development also included writing rubrics for the Literacy Passport Test. These rubrics were then used for improving writing instruction.

Mathematics was another focus of staff development. Two consultants provided the faculty with a number of math in-service opportunities. A few teachers said that new regulations affecting the special education were being put into effect and they participated in training to implement those regulations. Finally, one teacher took advantage of programs for parents offered by the Title I teacher, saying,

> She did a poetry workshop and I went to that. She has a lot of things within the school and within the community to help parents teach the kids better on how to read. I go to all those things.

Parent Involvement

The third goal of Timber Mountain Elementary's schoolwide plan was to increase parent involvement, a goal consistent with research literature that indicates parental involvement appears to account for 10-20% of the variance in student achievement (Thorkildsen & Stein, 1998). In addition to the programs offered by the Title I teacher, the school employed a home-school coordinator whose assignment was to teach parents how to help their children with schoolwork at home. She also conducted home visits and made recommendations for improving student performance.

The district supported increased parent involvement at the school level by employing a parent liaison coordinator who was paid through Title I. In addition, she had an aide, who was paid using a combination of other funds available to the district. Another district initiative, a career education center at the high school, served K-12 students as well as parents of K-12 students.

Although the school's plan was to increase parent involvement, the faculty's attitude toward parents and families was not consistent with a belief that parent involvement was important. One teacher summed up the prevailing attitude:

> We have a tough row to hoe here. The home-school coordinator is in charge of contacting parents. If I have any problems with any of my students, as far as work or attendance, I contact the coordinator and she makes visits or gets on the phone. I think that's had some payoff. Again, we've got a group of students coming from parents who don't place a lot of importance on education.

When asked to describe the relationship between the school and parents, several parents' responses showed that they sensed the faculty's negative attitude. Some complained of a breakdown in communication. One parent observed, "I want to be very active and help and whatever I can do, but I have felt more in the way here than welcome." Another parent complained, "When it gets to an uncomfortable situation, communication seems to shut down. For example, we definitely have lice in this school, and it's been three weeks and no notes have gone home." She continued,

> On a positive note, I did not know how to approach the school on a certain issue and the principal's response was, "How can we help?" That's the first time I ever heard of a school that did not have all the answers. I appreciated that because so often we parents are told, "We are the educators; we know everything."

However, several parents expressed concerns about the principal. One parent commented that ,

> While he seemed genuinely interested, when he looked into [my complaint] and called me to respond, he just said that teachers had been doing it that way for years. I don't feel that it's all right to continue something that is wrong just because you've always done it that way.

Parents also complained that they were not included in making decisions that affected them and their children. According to one parent,

> When the kindergarten was overcrowded, the school shifted teachers around to create a K-1 classroom without getting parent input. By the time they involve parents, the decision has already been made.

Another parent described discussions about scheduling a spring awards ceremony as "contentious." Parents were unhappy with the final decision. One explained,

> The faculty wanted the awards ceremony to be during the day because so many parents would not be able to bring their children back to school at night. The PTA voted to sponsor an awards program at night, but the faculty got together and voted us down. It's our money that is supporting it. To me that's wrong, because I think the parents develop successful children, not the school. Parents cannot get off work to attend the program during the school day. We try very hard to support our children.

Parent interactions with their child's teachers seemed to depend on individual teacher-parent relationships. Parents who were satisfied commented, "I think the teachers are very easy to deal with," "The school still has a wonderful staff," and "I think we're superb in that area." But a parent who was unhappy said, "Last year was a phenomenally awful year. I think it was the teacher, and I'm getting ready to face the same problem again because my youngest child is moving up to that grade next year."

Several parents felt the school did not get the same treatment as others in the district. For example, one commented, "Politics at the county level keep us from making progress. The principal has to satisfy the school board. It's wrong for the school system to be that way, but I can't blame the principal for looking out for himself."

Opportunities for All Students to Meet State Standards
Another goal of the schoolwide plan was to provide opportunities for all students to meet state standards. Components of this goal included curriculum, instruction, assessment, the traditional pullout program, and small class size.

Curriculum. Research consistently shows that high-performing schools embrace high standards and keep a schoolwide focus on teaching and learning (Newmann & Wehlage, 1995; Marks & Louis, 1997; David, 1994). State standards also provide focus and coherence to state and local education systems (Schmoker & Marzano, 1999). A well-written curriculum communicates clear, commonly defined goals that are essential to improvement

(Rosenholtz, 1991). Finally, schools get better results when teachers collaboratively decide what to teach by setting clear, common, manageable learning goals (Schmoker & Marzano, 1999).

Most importantly, alignment of curriculum, instruction, and assessment accounts for 50% of the variance in student academic performance (Cohen, 1995). Alignment is more powerful than socioeconomic status, gender, or teacher bias for predicting results on standardized tests (Wishnick, 1989), and alignment can also overcome differences in race and school size (Mitchell, 1998).

When Timber Mountain Elementary teachers were asked what curriculum they used, all of them responded that they taught the Virginia Standards of Learning (SOLs). The SOLs in Virginia were developed grade by grade, and are what the teachers relied on when deciding what to teach. Teachers began addressing SOLs early in the year so that students would be ready for the SOL test. Every week teachers chose skills to teach according to the SOLs, and record in their lesson plan books which SOLs had been taught. Since the SOLs for each grade build on the previous years' SOLs, teachers tried to ensure that students learned the requisite skills to be ready for the next grade. They were not always successful in this quest, however.

Teachers did not have a way to address the prerequisite skills students needed in order to learn the new content required by the standards. As one teacher explained, "It makes it difficult for students who are not on grade level. If we're adding fractions and the students don't know adding" those students are left behind.

When asked if they used the same curriculum with all students, teachers responded that generally they did. However, if the Title I teacher used a particular book with at-risk students, the regular classroom teacher would also use the same book with those students.

Instructional strategies. Teachers found that student achievement levels varied widely within their classrooms. For example, one teacher explained that although student reading levels in her home room ranged from the seventh grade to pre-primer level, she tended to teach to the highest ability level. Faced with this disparity, teachers decided to group students homogeneously by achievement level for English/language arts and math instruction.

To determine students' group placement, teachers began the school year by giving the Individual Reading Inventory (IRI), reviewing students' Stanford 9 scores, and giving a test constructed like the SOL test. Teachers explained that every 6 weeks, they reviewed student progress and made changes in placement if needed. Usually one or two students per grade level would be changed. Sometimes parent requests for changes were also considered. Changes in math groupings and English/language arts groupings were made independently.

Once the students were grouped within the grade level, one teacher would teach the high achievers in English/language arts and the low achievers in math. The other teacher in the same grade level would teach the high achievers in math and the low achievers in English/language arts. Teachers said they would rather have the same students all day every day; however, they believed that grouping the students was better for children than tracking students in a high or low group and assigning them to one teacher for the entire day.

The schoolwide program did not appear to have much impact on teaching strategies used by classroom teachers to boost student academic performance. One teacher indicated that she tried to be more intensive with her strategies. She worked with other teachers using a trial-and-error approach "to try to find out what works." Another said, "I work one-on-one with at-risk students, and that helps. I also use a lot of manipulatives and visuals. I had my students in groups once, but it didn't work."

Most teachers responded that the schoolwide program had not changed anything, although one teacher believed that there was "more Title I stuff going on in the primary schools."

Student assessment. When asked about classroom assessment, teachers indicated that a team of teachers had developed district level benchmarks.

> We have countywide benchmarks and the children have to master these benchmarks—or we hope they will master them. We also have grade-level meetings and meet with other grade levels to discuss what students should know before they go on to the next grade. The county works hard to make sure we have the assessment tools. We have benchmark cards and we keep up with them throughout the year. Hope-

> fully, when we mark it, the student has mastered it
> and when they get to the next grade, they will remem-
> ber it, but there is a lot of loss over the summer.

The benchmarks were the school's and district's response to the
state's new SOLs. Interviewed parents were aware of the benchmarks and understood that students had to meet a certain percentage of the benchmarks in order to move to the next grade level.

The schoolwide program, however, appeared to have little
impact on the way the teachers assessed student performance. One
teacher explained,

> The schoolwide program has not changed the way I
> assess students. I do a lot of re-teaching. We give
> quizzes and tests. Sometimes you just know the ones
> that are mastering skills. I give a lot of quizzes. That's
> mostly how I evaluate them. I usually don't wait until
> the end if the chapter. I evaluate each lesson. At the
> end of the unit, we review and make sure they have
> grasped and mastered the lessons. At the end of the
> chapter, we give a big test on the units.

Another teacher, who said that she had learned a lot about
assessment from the Title I teacher, was the exception. She
explained,

> The Title I teacher is one of my mentors. At the
> beginning of the year when she came in to do Individ-
> ual Reading Inventory, I learned a whole lot from
> her– how to look at reading to see if they actually are
> reading, not just looking at the words and calling out
> words. She talks to me about my kids that go to her,
> about what they are, and what they are not, doing that
> they should be doing. Also, we correct their home-
> work every day. They do a lot of board work. I watch
> to see how consistent they are. I just watch them a
> whole lot.

Traditional Pullout Program. Despite a commitment to
provide Title I services schoolwide, most of the school's Title I
funds supported the traditional pullout program. While other
primary schools in the district decided to use their Title I funds to
hire teacher aides, Timber Mountain Elementary chose to keep
their Title I teacher, who had been at the school prior to the
implementation of a schoolwide program. They also hired an aide

to assist her. During year one of schoolwide implementation, the school tried a classwide program in which the Title I teacher worked with the entire class, but teachers agreed that the results were unsatisfactory. One teacher explained,

> We saw that [at-risk students] were getting left behind. The instruction kept moving on for the others that were ready, but the at-risk never got anything that was on their level because it just kept going and going and going.

Therefore, in year two teachers at Timber Mountain Elementary decided to reinstate the traditional pullout program for K-3 students who needed intensive reading instruction. Through this strategy students assigned to the Title I teacher for a portion of the day were to receive more one-on-one instruction. Classroom teachers identified the students they believed "really need extra help" and assigned them to the Title I teacher one hour each day for intensive reading instruction. Title I classes lasted forty-five minutes and were held on a stage located at one end of the cafeteria. The Title I teacher scheduled time each day with groups of students, grade by grade. While the pullout program may have helped individual students who were assigned to it, it did not appear to affect the rest of the school program.

Of the 10 parents who were interviewed, however, there was general understanding that Title I emphasized reading skills. One parent expressed disappointment that the program no longer included math instruction. Parents also understood that it was a pullout program for children who were recommended by the classroom teacher. They believed that the children in Title I enjoyed a smaller class size and more one-on-one teaching than in the regular classroom allowing the teacher to be more focused on individual children. In contrast, they thought that the regular classrooms had too many children, but the teachers were doing the best that they could.

Small class size. The school also used several sources of funds to keep class sizes small. Small class size has long been thought to improve student achievement (Finn & Achilles, 1999). Timber Mountain Elementary also maintained smaller class sizes in the regular classroom. Because it has a high concentration of at-risk students, it received state funds through K-3 initiative to lower class size. Class size ranged from a low of 19 in kindergarten and Grade 1 to a high of 24 in Grade 5 (see Table 3). While there is evidence to support small class size as a way to improve performance, it has been shown to be a very expensive strategy, and one that works best when the teacher adopts new instructional strategies. Teachers at Timber Mountain Elementary, however, tended to select instructional strategies such as moving at a slower pace through the material or using less challenging material to meet the diverse needs of students.

Table 3.Class Size at Timber Mountain Elementary

Grade	Class Size
Pre-K	16
Kindergarten	19
First	19
Second	20
Third	22
Fourth	21
Fifth	24

Instructional time. Effective schools make good use of class time (Lezotte, 1995). According to the district's web site, Timber Mountain Elementary sets aside large blocks of time for mathematics and English/language arts at each grade level. When teachers were asked how they allocated time in their classroom, their responses were consistent with the district's expectation that the majority of class time was to be spent on English/language arts and math. Most teachers said that they usually spent at least two hours each day on English/language arts instruction and an hour and a half on math. Science and social studies were allotted a combined total of 45 minutes in the afternoon.

In addition to providing classroom instruction, resource personnel in art, music, media, and physical education work with each grade level to stimulate creative, academic, and physical achievement. Students also had a computer class three times a week in a new computer lab at the school. The computer class helped students learn computer skills required by the state standards and complemented the use of computers within the classrooms. Teachers observed that the daily instructional schedule was "very long and very busy." And, as one teacher indicated, "if the students have a really nice day, which has only happened about six times this year, then we go outside for a little while. Otherwise, we don't have time."

The variety of instructional opportunities plus the homogeneous grouping of students for English/language arts and math required students to change classrooms frequently. Not only did frequent class changes waste instructional time, it also had a detrimental effect on the creation of an orderly, safe climate conducive to teaching and learning—an important factor in creating effective schools (Lezotte, 1995).

Pre-school Program
    Project F.O.U.R. (Fostering Our Unique Resources), a program for at-risk four-year-olds, was another major component of Timber Mountain Elementary's schoolwide Title I program. This project was not new to the school or district. According to the district Title I coordinator, with the decrease in federal funds and the flexibility provided through the schoolwide initiative, the district "decided to put the Title I funds at Timber Mountain Elementary for the [Project F.O.U.R.] program, because Timber Mountain Elementary had a higher poverty rate than the other primary schools." In addition, the coordinator reported,

> Some have been unhappy with the . . . program, because we don't provide transportation. But the lack of transportation required parents to have twice-daily contact with the school. The Parenting Center is right next to the classroom door, so parents could easily check out videos or books. We've had some real success stories. We've had parents who finished their GED, connected with the local community college and found they could attend tuition free, and graduated with two-year degrees. Now, we've hired them as teacher aides.

Classroom teachers and the coordinator believed Project F.O.U.R. was successful. To document the success of the program, the district coordinator has tracked the progress of students who were enrolled in the program. She reported,

The first group is now in the fifth grade. We found
that only about one or two have problems and "fall
out" each year. So that leaves 97% on grade level.
They are very successful all the way through with
parental involvement.

Only two of ten parents who were interviewed knew that the
Project F.O.U.R. program was part of Title I. A parent explained
the purpose of the program:

The four-year-old program has helped children who
otherwise have no interaction with other children
until they start kindergarten. They need socialization
skills—how to sit and pay attention—and how to get
along with other children their own age. They get
used to a schedule—they go to school, it's time for
lunch, it's time to go outside. My son needs that.

Extended Learning Opportunities

As part of the Title I schoolwide plan, funds other than those
provided through Title I were used to provide activities and
services that complement the Title I program. Extended learning
opportunities include the homework club and developmental
learning center.

Homework Club. This program is an after-school homework
program helps third, fourth, and fifth graders complete homework
each day from 3:00 to 5:00 p.m. The district provides transporta-
tion home for those students who participate. Students mainly get
help with English/language arts and math but also receive some
help with science, social studies, preparing for tests, or completing
homework.

One parent was thankful for the "homework club," because
her son had difficulty getting his homework done. With the
homework club, he could "stay and not have the distractions that
go on at home." The parent thought that the program had helped
him to bring up his grades tremendously.

Another parent said simply the "homework program works."
She worked with a classroom teacher to set up a program with
study guides for students who were struggling but not participating
in the homework program. She added, "After talking with the
parents, they agreed to let their children enter the homework

program, and all three children got an A in social studies on their next report card."

Developmental Learning Center. According to the district Title I coordinator, the Developmental Learning Center helped extend the adult and parent training opportunities, as part of the district's consolidated plan to coordinate and leverage federal dollars. All the federally funded initiatives have a literacy thrust—student, family, and adult literacy. Flexibility with use of funds also made it possible to get GED Test preparation tapes.

One parent described the Developmental Learning Center as "open to anybody." "A parent just has to come with the children up through the third grade. Parents help children with homework and then participate in a class to talk about parenting." Another parent observed, "If parents would come with their children, they would learn how to put them in the right environment for studying and establish good study habits so they can study on their own." Another parent commented, "My second grader hates homework. The Developmental Learning Center taught me how to help. She wants it to be quiet, no television; she has to have a certain setting for doing her homework."

The Big Three: Leadership, Vision, and Collaboration

Leadership

Principal leadership is an important characteristic in schools found to be more effective (Lezotte, 1995). Timber Mountain Elementary's principal was new to both the school and to the role of principal. He was observed spending much of his time behind closed doors with parents discussing the discipline of their child. He frequently interrupted classroom instruction to make announcements over the intercom. In addition, he did not appear to monitor instruction closely to ensure that the new state standards were implemented.

Most of the parents' reactions to the new principal, however, were positive. One parent commented that if she had a problem or a question, it was easy to get an answer; another agreed that parents had ready access to the principal. A third parent was pleased that the principal was sending a newsletter home for the first time.

Vision

Schools which are more successful also tend to have a pervasive and broadly understood vision (Lezotte, 1995; Wehlage & Newmann, 1995). According to the Title I coordinator, the district had developed a vision statement, which was "to provide a safe environment in which all students are prepared with the thinking skills necessary to function as self-disciplined, productive learners."

When teachers at Timber Mountain Elementary were asked about the vision of the school, however, there was little agreement among their responses. Several mentioned the SOLs. One teacher responded that the vision was to educate children. Another teacher was more specific, saying that the goal for Title I was to have all children reading on grade level by third grade. She added, "I know that's a vision; I know it hasn't been reached in this school." One respondent voiced a child-centered vision:

> The vision is to teach the kids in a secure, loving environment where they don't have to be scared to come to school, where they can talk to anybody if they have a problem, to teach them at the level they need to be taught at, the way they need to be taught. If they need lecturing, we'll lecture them; if they need hands-on, we do hands-on. We talk to them the way we would want to be talked to; to treat them the same way; to be role models; to help them be the best, well-rounded person they can be.

Parents who were interviewed responded that they were not aware of any formal goals or vision statement associated with the school. One parent said, "I hope it is to educate our children." Another expressed hope that the vision was for "the safety, welfare, and education of our children."

Collaboration

Collaboration has been found to be an important component of successful school restructuring (Newmann & Wehlage, 1995). True collaborative activity increases the likelihood that teachers will share goals and reinforce similar objectives, improve their technical competence, and share responsibility for student learning.

Little collaborative activity occurred at Timber Mountain Elementary. However, teachers who taught the same grade level frequently shared information and materials. One pair of grade-level teachers indicated that they had attended a reading conference and shared information with the faculty. In addition, the pair talked about and were trying to use literature circles, after one of them acquired information about them from a conference.

Other teachers offered that if they did not have a teacher edition of a textbook, they would borrow one from another teacher. If they did not have enough textbooks, they would also circulate them. Teachers who taught the same grade would get together and discuss what they were doing so students in that grade could do about the same thing and work on the same skills. For example, one teacher said she got all the materials for *Charlotte's Web* from one of the other teachers. Another said that since she was a first-year teacher, she found she needed to get ideas and materials from other teachers.

Overall, teachers indicated that there was not much time for collaboration and that collaboration was not valued by the staff or the administration. Teachers thought it was beneficial that the principal had worked that teachers at each grade level had the same 45-minute planning time. There was no expectation that teachers would spend that time collaborating, and most indicated they used the time to "run off papers or finish report cards or things like that." As one teacher said,

> You're lucky if you have time to grade your papers or go to the [copy] machine let alone think about what you're going to teach. We have planning four days a week. It's supposed to be 45 minutes, but by the time the person comes to the room and gets the kids, it's cut down to 35-40.

Some teachers who wanted to collaborate chose to stay after school. One teacher explained,

> I don't leave school until about 6 p.m. That's how we do it. The three third-grade teachers are here and have a chance to discuss and talk and plan strategies that are helpful. Because of the grouping of students, we talk about how children are doing and responding in different teachers' classes. We share knowledge about the computer, like how to make puzzles for spelling.

While teachers' responses suggested a high degree of collegiality, there was little evidence of schoolwide planning and teamwork. For example, the schoolwide plan called for a school-wide improvement team at Timber Mountain Elementary, but the coordinator was uncertain about its existence, saying,

> Hopefully, we've got a schoolwide improvement team in place. Hopefully, that team is meeting on a regular basis. It includes parents, regular education teachers, the Title I teacher, the principal, and who-ever needs to be invited. The school improvement team is organized using the guidelines from IDEA [Individuals with Disabilities Education Act] for Child Find and child screening. This process puts a lot of effort and energy into designing an individual child's plans.

At the school level, teachers who were interviewed did not mention a schoolwide improvement team. One parent mentioned that the school had a school improvement team that was supposed to meet once a month but usually met every two months. Another didn't know there was such a committee, and another knew there was a committee but had never heard about anything that occurred at the meetings. One parent asked who served on the committee, and another asked how people got the committee. The parent who served on the team said he had been appointed by the principal.

Conclusions

The findings at Timber Mountain Elementary suggest several fallacies of thought at the district and school levels that contrib-uted to the school's implementation of an improvement plan in name only. District politics appeared to lead to programs that were fragmented, and the school did not have a coherent vision. The principal provided minimal leadership for improving the quality of instruction. Teacher planning, professional develop-ment, and curriculum were fragmented. Although teachers were very aware of the new state standards, there was little collabora-tion or discussion about how the school could work to develop a curriculum aligned with state standards. Under district leadership, teachers had developed benchmarks that articulated what students should know at the end of each grade level, but they had not developed classroom assessments to measure student progress toward those benchmarks throughout the school year.

Timber Mountain Elementary had received Title I funds that seemed sufficient to adopt a major comprehensive reform program. But, even when used in conjunction with other federal funds, the school chose to use those funds to continue a traditional pullout program which benefitted only a few students. The use of smaller class size, a strategy funded by the state and instituted by the district, might have been more effective if teachers were also using proven instructional strategies.

There is no evidence to suggest that homogeneous grouping, the primary strategy chosen by regular classroom teachers, has promise for improving student performance. In fact, this type of grouping often "affects students in ways contrary to teachers' intentions" (Oakes, 1985, p. 5). Further, grouping students resulted in students being taught by several different teachers during the school day, which made it difficult for classroom teachers to develop strong relationships with students, an important contributor to improved student learning (Comer, Haynes, Joyner, & Ben-Avie, 1996). Grouping students also required frequent class changes that decreased instructional time instead of maximizing it. At best, the Homework Club, supervised after-school study time, helped to make up for time lost during the school day, but it did so at extra cost.

One of Timber Mountains' stated goals was increased parent involvement with the school. Teacher comments, however, about students who were difficult to teach and families who did not value education revealed negative attitudes toward parents. Parents' comments about their own relationship with the school revealed mixed feelings.

Timber Mountain Elementary's original goal was to improve student learning by implementing a schoolwide improvement plan. Unfortunately, the introduction of new tests during the school's first year of implementation prevents a close comparison of "before and after" scores, although the school did perform below expectations under the new testing system as well. It can also be said that the eight goals stated in the school's improvement plan focus on discrete activities, not on integrating and coordinating these activities for specific learning results. The goals in no way constitute a vision for the school. Lack of a compelling vision, strong leadership, and teacher collaboration kept Timber Mountain Elementary from discovering whether a truly comprehensive improvement plan might have put the school "back on track."

References

Burczyk, R. (1998). *1995-96 locale types (Johnson codes): Designation for schools in AEL's region.* Charleston, WV: AEL, Inc.

Ceperley, P. (1999). *Implementation of Title I schoolwide programs in four rural Virginia schools.* Paper presented at the annual meeting of the American Educational Research Association, Montreal, Canada.

Cohen, S. A. (1995). Instructional alignment. In J. H. Block, S. T. Everson, and T. R. Guskey (Eds.), *School Improvement Programs* (pp. 153-180). New York: Scholastic, Inc.

Comer, J. P., Haynes, N. M., Joyner, E. T., & Ben-Avie, B. (1996). *Rallying the whole village: The Comer process for reforming education.* New York: Teachers College Press.

David, J. L. (1994). *School-based decision making: Linking decisions to learning. Third year report to the Pritchard Committee.* Palo Alto, CA: Bay Area Research Group.

Finn, J. & Achilles, C. (1999). Tennessee's class size study: Findings, implications, misconceptions. *Educational Evaluation and Policy Analysis, 21* (2), 97-110.

Lezotte, L. W. (1995). Effective schools: The evolving research and practices. In J. H. Block, S. T. Everson, & T. R. Guskey (Eds.), *School improvement programs* (pp. 313-342). New York: Scholastic.

Marks, H. M. & Louis, K. S. (1997). Does teacher empowerment affect the classroom? The implications of teacher empowerment for instructional practice and student academic performance. *Educational Evaluation and Policy Analysis, 19,* 245-275.

Mitchell, F. M. (1998). *The effects of curriculum alignment on the mathematics achievement of third-grade students as measured by the Iowa Tests of Basic Skills: Implications for educational administrators.* Unpublished dissertation, Clark Atlanta University, Atlanta, Georgia.

Newmann, F. M. & Wehlage, G. G. (1995). *Successful school restructuring: A report to the public and educators.* Madison, WI: Center on Organization and Restructuring of Schools, University of Wisconsin-Madison, School of Education, Wisconsin Center for Education Research.

Oakes, J. (1985). *Keeping track—How schools structure inequality.* New Haven, CT: Yale University Press.

Rosenholtz, S. J. (1991). *Teacher's workplace: The social organization of schools.* New York: Teachers College Press.

Schmoker, M. & Marzano, R. (1999). Realizing the promise of standards-based education. *Education Leadership, 56,* 6, 17-21.

Stapleton, P. (1998). *Governor's Best Practice Centers.* Richmond, VA: Virginia Department of Education. Unpublished position paper.

Thorkildsen, R. & Stein, M. R. S. (1998, December). Is parent involvement related to student achievement? Exploring the evidence. *Phi Delta Kappa Research Bulletin,* 22, 17-20.

Wang, M. C., Wong, K. K., & Kim, J. (1999). *A national study of Title I schoolwide programs: A synopsis of interim findings.* Philadelphia: Temple University, Laboratory for Student Success.

Wishnick, T. (1989). Relative effects on achievement scores of SES, gender, teacher affect and instructional alignment. *Dissertation Abstracts International, 51*(04A), 1107. (University Microfilms No. 9019604)

Wong, K. K. & Meyer, S. (1998). *An overview of Title I schoolwide programs: Federal legislative expectations.* Philadelphia: Temple University, Laboratory for Student Success.

Yancey, W. L., Breeding, C. and Freely, J. (1998). *Identifying exceptional schools in Virginia.* Unpublished manuscript, Temple University, Laboratory for School Success, Philadelphia.

CHAPTER 7

STRUGGLING WITH IMPLEMENTATION:
TWO SCHOOLWIDE PROGRAMS THAT DID
NOT MAKE A DIFFERENCE

Mary Helen S. McCoy & Thomasine Haskins Mencer

This chapter presents case studies of two elementary schools that were part of a multi-year, multi-school evaluation of Title I schoolwide programs. It is a companion to Chapter 4. The schoolwide program at these schools failed to improve student test scores or change teachers' instructional methods. They are a contrast to the two schools described in Chapter 4. They are located in a district which serves 56,000 students at schools located in urban, sub-urban, and rural areas. Other studies resulting from this evaluative research have been presented elsewhere (McCoy & Taylor, 1999; Taylor, Ratcliff, & Kemper, 1999; Taylor & Teddlie, 1999).

Data Collection Procedures

The two schools discussed in this chapter will be referred to by the pseudonyms, Lincoln Elementary and Madison Elementary. As Lincoln and Madison neared the end of their second year of participation in the Title I schoolwide program, a team of researchers visited to collect a variety of data.

Qualitative data were gathered several ways. Each school's Title I plan was analyzed to identify goals and strategies. Also, structured interviews were conducted with the principal and approximately one-third of the teachers. Interviewed teachers were selected using a stratified random sampling procedure to ensure that at least one teacher from each grade level was interviewed. An interview protocol was developed that probed for information about the contents of the Title I plan and its implementation. A final technique for collecting qualitative data was to script during classroom observations, which lasted approximately 30 minutes. These observations occurred in 50%-75% of the classrooms and included at least one class per grade level.

Quantitative data were also gathered during the classroom observations. An instrument called the Components of Effective Teaching (CET) had been developed and validated by the state in which the district was located. The CET assessed teaching quality in two domains, instruction and management. Response choices are arrayed Likert-style on a four point scale, ranging from 1 = "Unsatisfactory" to 4 = "Demonstrates Excellence." In addition, questionnaires were distributed to the principal, all teachers in each school and students in one randomly selected class at each grade level, third through fifth, per school. When possible, items on the questionnaires were worded so that responses could be compared between students and teachers.

Lincoln Elementary and Madison Elementary were chosen for this chapter because they provide examples of schools with ineffective Title I schoolwide programs. We present a case study of each school, including (a) an introductory section with demographics and student achievement information, (b) a discussion of the schoolwide plan, (c) an analysis of principal leadership, (d) findings regarding school climate, and (e) a case summary. We conclude our chapter with a discussion of the cases.

Lincoln Elementary School

Demographics and Student Achievement
Lincoln Elementary School, built in the late 1960s, stands amid mature trees in a quiet, working class community. The tidy, brick, single story building with a grassy yard and well-equipped play area, held promise of an inviting place for teaching and learning.

During the 1997-98 school year, approximately 417 students were enrolled at Lincoln in pre-K through fifth grades. A year before the research team visited Lincoln, the district redrew the attendance zones to enable elementary schools to draw their students from the surrounding neighborhoods. This decision, along with other causes of student transience, resulted in an approximately 75% change in the student population at the school. The Title I application at Lincoln showed that 99% of the youngsters were African-American, and state data indicate that 94% of the students received free or reduced-price lunch.

In contrast to the student body, the Lincoln faculty experienced very little turnover. In fact, 64% of the 37 teachers had taught at the school for five or more years. More than two-thirds of the professional staff had education beyond a Bachelor's degree. In addition to the certified staff, three aides, funded through Title I, worked at the school.

The principal, Ms. Carson, had been at the school for more than 10 years. She was in her mid-fifties and suffered with arthritis. As a result, she appeared to have great difficulty maneuvering around the school. The evaluation team noted that throughout their visit, Ms. Carson was not seen beyond the area surrounding her office.

As noted above, several of the professional staff were interviewed. In addition to the principal, eight others, including six regular teachers, the guidance counselor, and the Title I teacher, were interviewed about Lincoln's Title I plan. Questionnaires were returned by the principal, and 14 of the 37 teachers. The teacher return rate was low, particularly in comparison to other schools in the multi-year study. Fifty-six students from grades 3-5 also completed questionnaires

During the 1997-98 school year, when these data were collected, Lincoln, like other elementary schools in the district, felt the impact of a new norm-referenced test (NRT), the Iowa Test of Basic Skills (ITBS). The first year the ITBS was administered, students in grades 2 and 4 took the test. Lincoln youngsters scored within, or just above, the bottom quartile. Second graders scored at the 24th percentile in reading, the 15th percentile in mathematics, and the 15th percentile on the composite total. Fourth graders scored slightly higher with scores at the 21st percentile in reading, the 23rd percentile in mathematics, and the 26th percentile on the composite total. Even though changing NRTs sometimes depresses scores in the first year of administration, and Lincoln had experienced a large turnover of students, these scores are unacceptably low.

Students in third and fifth grades took a state administered criterion referenced test (CRT). CRT results were consistent with those from the NRT. The third grade attainment rates were 77% in language arts and 83% in mathematics, while the state average attainment rates for third graders were 90% in language arts and 88% in mathematics. Lincoln fifth grade students had an attainment rate of 69% in language arts compared to a statewide attainment rate of 85% in language arts; however in mathematics the fifth graders had an attainment rate of 87%, quite close to their peers' statewide attainment rate of 88%. These results suggest that there was a positive impact with fifth graders in mathematics, but that overall students demonstrated significant learning deficits.

The Schoolwide Plan

Lincoln received over $380,000 in Title I funds over the two years of its involvement in the schoolwide program. Among the goals established were: (1) raise achievement in reading and mathematics, (2) increase the use of technology in teaching and learning, (3) provide staff development, and (4) increase parental involvement. These four goals and the accompanying strategies are presented in Table 1.

Ms. Carson was interviewed about the schoolwide plan. She seemed apprehensive and reluctant to be interviewed, but described the Title I program as "very effective," and credited certain components of the program with enabling several students to be promoted to the next grade instead of retained. In describing the plan, Ms. Carson said that she throught it was more important for the children attending Lincoln to get extra attention from adults than to have additional instructional materials, such as computers. Even though increasing computer use was a goal of the Title I plan, she stated emphatically that she "didn't want computers, [she] wanted people." A budget analysis confirmed Ms. Carson's emphasis on people. It was estimated that 72% of the two-year total allocation was designated for Title I personnel. Even when the district substantially cut the school's Title I budget, Ms. Carson continued to allocate most of the Title I dollars to human resources, electing to reduce the number of Title I teachers from three to one, and to hire three aides. She spent very little on instructional materials.

Table 1. Goals and Strategies from Title I Plan at Lincoln Elementary School.

Goals
1. Increase achievement in reading and mathematics
2. Use technology in teaching and learning
3. Provide staff development
4. Increase parent involvement
Instruction strategies
1. Computers assisted instruction in reading and mathematics
2. Accelerated Reader Program
3. Reading Recovery strategies
4. Small group instruction
5. Thematic units
6. Hands-on activities/manipulatives
7. Collaborative teaching
Staff development
1. Computers, technology, and software
2. Cooperative grouping
3. Thematic units
4. Manipulatives
5. Collaborative planning
6. Team teaching
7. Problem solving
8. Test taking skills
9. Observation at other schools
10. Classroom management
Parent Involvement
1. Workshops
2. Parent room in the library
3. Families and Schools Together program
4. Parent Teacher Association
5. Monthly newsletter

Following the budget cut, the single remaining Title I teacher divided her time among the classroom teachers, working with two teachers each day. Faculty who were interviewed said they enjoyed working with the Title I specialist, commenting that "the Title I teacher was informative and knowledgeable and willing to help out with anything," and that "it's heaven sent to have assistance in the classroom." They noted that the additional teacher had the effect of lowering the adult-to-student ratio. However, neither the Title I teacher nor the regular teachers thought the new arrangement was particularly effective. Classroom observations corroborated those impressions.

Student achievement in reading and mathematics. A primary goal of Title I schools in the district was to raise test scores in reading and mathematics. At Lincoln, several instructional strategies were proposed to help achieve this goal. These strategies can be found in Table 1 and include such methods as small group instruction, thematic units, and hands-on activities. In addition, Title I teachers or aides were to work with the regular teachers during whole class and small group instruction when reading and mathematics were taught. Finally, time was provided weekly for collaborative planning at each grade level. These meetings included regular teachers, Title I personnel, and ancillary teachers, and helped to facilitate smooth interaction within the classroom. Class observation, however, suggested that this planning had little impact on introducing the specific teaching strategies called for in the Title I plan, though the Title I teachers and aides worked very well with the regular teachers during our classroom visits.

Eleven classes were visited to determine the extent to which the instructional goals were being implemented, and to provide an overall assessment of the quality of teaching at Lincoln. As reported in Table 2, lesson content in all 11 classes involved skill building and drill, with little attention given to higher order thinking. Students spent most of their class time copying from a blackboard or overhead projector, answering factual questions, waiting for other students to complete their work, and waiting until other students were assisted before getting help from the teacher. Small group instruction and hands-on activities, strategies specifically targeted in the Title I plan, were observed in only two classes. Unfortunately, the Accelerated Reader program, Reading Recovery strategies, and thematic units, also targeted in the Title I plan, were not observed in any classroom. Interestingly, given Ms. Carson's feelings about computers, students were observed using computers in four classes, as will be discussed in the next subsection.

Table 2. Number of Times Each Instructional Component of the Title I Plan was Observed in Eleven Classrooms at Lincoln Elementary

Program Component	Times Observed
Computer assisted instruction	4
Accelerated Reader Program	0
Reading Recovery strategies	0
Small group instruction	2
Thematic units	0
Hands-on activities/manipulatives	2
Collaborative teaching with Title I teacher	2
Skill building and drill	11
Higher order thinking skills	1

The Title I teacher was observed for 60-minutes, and the three Title I aides were observed for 30 minutes each. Additional data regarding Title I personnel were collected when the teacher or an aide happened to be in a classroom during an observation of a regular teacher. The observations indicated that Title I personnel were used primarily as monitors to curb disruptive behavior. The lack of instructional responsibilities assigned to Title I personnel prompted one evaluator to comment that the "Title I teacher acted more as a student-observer than a teacher." Occasionally the Title I teacher or aide did work with a group of students on activities such as writing tasks, telling time, or working with manipulatives.

Because classroom activities are integral to student learning, additional discussion of the findings from the observations is warranted. A warm environment was evident in several classes; however, the atmosphere was chaotic in many of the other classes. Routines and procedures were limited in several rooms where teachers struggled for control. In one kindergarten class, for example, a girl gained momentary silence when she yelled, "Shut up!" In another kindergarten class, students wandered around, and one boy meandered into an adjoining classroom without his absence being detected by the teacher. Teachers did not attempt to secure students' attention, as in one second grade class where the teacher tried to talk over the students. In the many instances such as these, teachers accommodated off-task behavior as the norm and maintained a neutral affect toward the students.

The scripting data from the observations, along with the quantitative data from the CET and the questionnaires, suggest that teachers had low expectations for students. The average score on the CET for the indicator "establishes expectations for learning behavior"(2.3) indicated that teachers' skills were weak in this area. Further, on the questionnaire, half of the teachers, as well as the principal, marked that students at the school were low in ability. The conclusion we drew as researchers was that the chaos observed at the school was tolerated by the adults because they did not believe the students were capable of better behavior.

Table 3 illustrates teacher performance on the CET. The average score for instructional indicators was 2.3, and the average score for management indicators was 2.4, both of which were below the midpoint of 2.5. These results suggest that teachers needed much additional staff development. The lowest CET scores were on the indicators "stimulates and encourages higher order thinking" (1.7), "accommodates individual differences" (1.8), "adjusts lesson when appropriate" (1.9), and "uses techniques which develop lesson effectively" (1.9).

Despite the chaotic atmosphere in the classrooms and the weak CET scores, most teachers expressed a strong sense of efficacy. Of the teachers responding to the questionnaire, 78% indicated that there was much they could do to insure high student achievement. Why they were not doing so was not discovered during the school visit, but should become a topic of staff discussions regarding school improvement. A much smaller 21% of the teachers felt they were limited in bringing about high levels of student achievement.

Use of Technology in Teaching and Learning. Although not prevalent, computer use was the most frequently observed instructional component of the Title I program. In four of the 11 classes visited, a total of ten students were observed using computers. Instructional activities undertaken by these students

Table 3. Lincoln Elementary Mean Scores on the CET.

Indicators by Domain	Mean
Instructional Indicators	2.3
Uses techniques which develop lesson effectively	1.9
Sequences lesson to promote learning	2.5
Uses available materials to achieve lesson objectives	2.3
Adjusts lesson when appropriate	1.9
Presents content at developmentally appropriate level	2.6
Presents accurate subject matter	3.1
Relates relevant examples...or events to content	2.2
Accommodates individual differences	1.8
Communicates effectively with students	2.3
Stimulates and encourages higher order thinking	1.7
Encourages student participation	2.6
Monitors on-going performance of students	2.1
Provides feedback to students regarding their progress	2.6
Management Indicators	2.4
Organizes space, materials, equipment to facilitate learning	2.8
Promotes a positive learning climate	2.4
Manages routines/transitions in timely manner	2.5
Manages/adjusts time for planned activities	2.2
Establishes expectations for learning behavior	2.3
Uses monitoring to facilitate learning	2.1

Note: Scores are as follows: 1=Unsatisfactory; 2=Improvement; 3=Area of Strength; 4= Demonstrates Excellence. The midpoint of the scale is 2.5

included writing book reports and creating post card fronts. The computers were not always used to enhance instruction, however. Often teachers used time at the computer as a reward for completing work. For example, in one class where the computers were covered with plastic, the teacher announced that the computers would be turned on for those who behaved and finished their paper and pencil assignment.

Staff Development. Staff development was one of the goals targeted in the Title I plan. The School Support Team proposed for staff development the ten topics listed in Table 1. Eight of the topics were directly related to the enhancement of instruction and student achievement and consistent with the instructional strategies included in the Title I plan. Topics such as computers, cooperative grouping, thematic units, and manipulatives should have facilitated the implementation of the instructional strategies proposed in the schoolwide plan. Only 2% of the Title I budget was allocated for staff development at Lincoln; these funds were to provide presenters, consultants, incentives, and refreshments. The staff development effort appeared to be marginally effective, although six of the eight teachers who were interviewed said that they participated in staff development activities. According to these teachers, staff development topics included computer technology, reading and mathematics strategies, use of manipulatives, collaborative planning, test taking skills, and observations at other schools. When queried about these activities, however, the teachers had trouble remembering specifics, and they were unable to elaborate on ways they implemented what was presented. Another indicator that staff development was not effective at Lincoln came from the teacher questionnaire. While 85% of the teachers responding to the questionnaire felt the staff development activities would enhance their teaching, only 15% thought the quality of the activities was high compared to other schools.

Parent Involvement. The School Support Team believed that increased parent involvement would help insure student success, improve the school climate, and improve discipline. Therefore, the Title I plan proposed a number of activities that are listed in Table 1. One activity was parent workshops conducted by local community service agencies (e.g., public health agencies, mental health agencies, parenting centers) and by Lincoln's guidance counselor, school nurse, visiting teacher, and principal. Communications between the school and students' homes were to be facilitated by a special program, Families and Schools Together, and by frequent newsletters. Also, plans were made to establish a place in the library where parents could read, use computers, and learn strategies for helping their children with homework.

When asked about Lincoln's parents, the interviewed teachers believed that parent involvement was "good, but could be better." One teacher stated that parent involvement "has improved because of the Town Meeting (a planning session required by the school board at each elementary school), monthly programs, and parent workshops." No one mentioned parent use of the library as called for in the plan.

Teacher responses to questionnaire items about parent involvement reflect more limited involvement than was described in the interviews. In contrast to the comments teachers made during interviews, a small 14% of the teachers agreed that parent involvement in activities at the school was frequent. If parent involvement were limited, as indicated by this response, it may explain why only 57% of these elementary school teachers indicated that they knew most of the parents of their student when they saw them. Not knowing the parents may also account for finding that just 36% of the teachers believed that the parents cared about their children's grades.

Principal Leadership

As indicated in Table 4, Ms. Carson's opinions as to her leadership of Lincoln Elementary differed with those of the teachers. Ms. Carson saw herself as a supportive administrator who protected instructional time, readily assisted in improving the instructional program, and included teachers in decision making. She believed that she was visible and available throughout the school, and did a good job of getting resources for the school.

Although the teachers appeared to like Ms. Carson, they did not view her leadership in as positive a light. Less than one-third of the teachers strongly agreed that Ms. Carson protected instructional time, while only 21% felt it was easy to get her assistance in improving instruction. Perhaps the largest disparity between the perceptions of the teachers and Ms. Carson was her visibility throughout the school. Surprisingly, Ms. Carson strongly agreed that she was visible schoolwide, but only 7% of the teachers expressed the same opinion, corroborating the experiences of the research team during their visit to Lincoln.

Table 4. Comparison of Perceptions of the Principal's Leadership at Lincoln Elementary

Leadership indicator	Principal's Perception	Percentage of Teachers Agreeing with the Principal
Principal protects instructional time	Strongly agreed	29%
Principal assists teachers' efforts to improve instruction	Strongly agreed	21%
Principal emphasizes teachers' involvement in decision making	Agreed	57%
Principal is visible throughout the school	Strongly agreed	7%
Principal does a good job of getting resources to the school	Strongly agreed	36%
Principal supports teachers' disciplinary efforts	Strongly agreed	21%
Principal consistently enforces discipline policy	Agreed	36%

The indicator on which Ms. Carson and the faculty were in closest agreement was involving the teachers in decision making. Over half of the teachers shared Ms. Carson's perception that teachers were included in decision making. With regard to disciplinary matters, Ms. Carson felt strongly that she was supportive of teachers, though only 21% of the teachers also indicated strong agreement. Ms. Carson realized that she was not consistent with discipline, but still gave herself a relatively high rating; only 36% of the teachers agreed.

Unlike the teachers, who maintained some sense of efficacy in the face of evidence to the contrary, Ms. Carson reported that she had only "some effect" on student achievement and on teachers' ability to teach effectively. Sadly, she did not feel that there was much she could do to insure high student achievement, nor did she believe that with the cooperation of the faculty, she could change Lincoln into a high achieving school. Unfortunately, Ms. Carson had lost confidence in herself, a dilemma that affected both the campus and classroom climate at Lincoln.

School Climate

Ms. Carson believed Lincoln was a good place for teaching and learning. On the questionnaire, she marked that the school was safe for students and teachers, a perception with which approximately three-fourths of the teachers and students agreed. While the teachers indicated on the questionnaire that they thought Lincoln provided an orderly environment, 82% of the students said their class was often disrupted by unruly students.

Students' perceptions of school climate were probed through an open-ended item on the questionnaire that asked them to list the best and worst things about Lincoln. Teachers were listed as one of the best things by 31 students, but 27 also named recess and other breaks from class. The worst thing about Lincoln was "bad kids" who talked back to the teachers and picked on other students. Nineteen students mentioned this problem, while another 14 listed fighting as a problem. The comment of one student about misbehavior reflected the sentiments of others, "Lincoln has a lot of violence. They have too many fights, and, too much talking back." A third topic named by students as one of the worst things about the school was specific subjects, which ten students named. While some students at every school in the multi-year study named specific subjects as among the worst things about their school, at no other school was this complaint in the top three.

These findings suggest a noteworthy difference between the opinions of the professional staff and the students regarding the climate of the school. There were indications during the visit, noted by members of the research team, that the principal and teachers tried to cast the school in as positive light as possible. Teachers' perceptions may be more accurately reflected in their response to an item asking if they would transfer to another school if given the choice. Forty-three percent of the teachers said they would leave, and another 14% indicated they were unsure.

Summary of Lincoln Elementary

Lincoln Elementary School made marginal gains toward implementation of the Title I schoolwide program. The human resources made possible through Title I, and deemed important by the principal, were underutilized. Staff development activities made little impression on the teachers and resulted in little carryover into the classroom.

Perhaps these problems existed because the Title I program was undermined by weak teaching and poor leadership. Classroom observations revealed that weak classroom management frequently interfered with instructional time; however, this problem was not addressed by Ms. Carson. Adding to the problems, Ms. Carson did not view the Title I plan as an integral part of the school. Rather, Title I was kept separate from the regular instructional program, causing her to seek Title I funding without a sense that the school should, or could, improve because of it. Most problematic at Lincoln was the low sense of efficacy expressed by the principal. The principal's inability to imagine Lincoln as a successful school under her leadership had a cascading effect that minimized teachers' effort and kept test scores at the school low.

Madison Elementary School

Demographics and Student Achievement

Madison Elementary School is located in a quiet, low-income community. Built in 1964, this school consisted of 16 permanent classrooms in single-story, low-roofed buildings situated on a well-kept, 9.5-acre tract of land. At the time the research team visited, the facility was clean but in general disrepair. The principal, Ms. Denny, explained that although maintenance personnel were keeping up the best they could, the facility badly needed a new roof. She explained that when it rained, buckets were strategically placed around the school to protect the carpeting. Other than some routine maintenance, the only improvements over the years were a library renovation in the 1960s and the addition of air conditioning in the early 1970s.

Ms. Denny was in her first year as principal at Madison. She stated that during that year she had found that those in the semi-rural community in which the school was located did not particularly value education, but that the residents placed great value on the school as a community institution. Furthermore, according to Ms. Denny, neither the school nor the community had changed substantially during her predecessor's 20-year tenure at the school. She described expectations for learning at Madison as generally low.

At the time of the site visit, approximately 300 students in pre-K through fifth grades attended Madison. The Title I plan described the student population as predominately African-American (97%) and economically deprived (95%). Student attendance rates, however, were satisfactory, with an average daily attendance rate of 97%. Many of the students at Madison were new to the school. Only 43% of students aged 8 to 12 years had been at the school more than two years. The faculty was a bit more stable. Of the faculty who returned questionnaires, 38% had been at the school for ten or more years, and another 13% had been there for at least five years.

Data at Madison were collected in the same manner as at Lincoln. The principal and eight of the 14 regular education teachers at the school were interviewed. In addition, observations were conducted in seven classrooms. Finally, questionnaires were returned by the principal, by eight teachers, and by 59 students in the third, fourth, and fifth grades.

As at Lincoln Elementary School, the standardized test performance of Madison students was weak. In 1997-1998, students in grades 2 and 4 took the Iowa Test of Basic Skills (ITBS). As previously noted, this was the first year that the ITBS was used by the district as the norm-referenced test (NRT) and scores may be somewhat depressed as a result. Nonetheless, Madison students performed in the bottom quartile. Second grade students scored at the 23rd percentile in reading, at the 25th percentile in mathematics, and at the 20th percentile on composite total. Performance of students in the fourth grade was worse. These students scored at the 15th percentile in reading, at the 22nd percentile in mathematics, and at the 20th percentile on the composite total.

Students in grades 3 and 5 likewise performed poorly on the state criterion-referenced test (CRT), with attainment levels well below state averages. Third grade attainment rates of 73% in language arts and 77% in mathematics were down by five to six percentage points from the previous year, and substantially below the state average attainment rates of 90% and 88% in language arts and mathematic, respectively. For fifth grade students, the language arts attainment rate of 76% represented an increase of 16 percentage points over the prior year, but the mathematics attainment rate of 59% was down by eight percentage points. These scores are below the state averages of 85% and 88% in language arts and mathematics, respectively.

The Schoolwide Plan

During the two-year period of schoolwide program participation, Madison received over $240,000 in Title I funding. The school's overall Title I plan was complicated, utilizing 29 strategies to satisfy four goals aimed at instruction, technology usage, staff development, and parent involvement. Table 5 presents a summary of the goals and the accompanying strategies.

To Ms. Denny, the most important components of the Title I plan were computers, the Reading Recovery program, heterogeneous multi-age groups, staff development, and parent involvement. She described how funding from various sources had been used to provide academic support across grade levels, mentioning that needed materials such as supplemental math materials, computer software, dictionaries, desks, and chairs had been purchased through a composite of federal funds.

Ms. Denny inherited the Madison Title I plan from her predecessor and had no input in its formulation. Perhaps because of this limited involvement, she seemed a little apprehensive about the site visit. Still, her support of the plan was obvious. The faculty shared her positive attitude toward the schoolwide plan and felt improvements were being made in student learning. The following subsections describe evidence about strategies implemented to achieve the Title I goals that relate to instruction, staff development, technology, and parent involvement.

Achievement in language arts and mathematics. Title I personnel at Madison worked alongside regular classroom teachers to provide students with academic support in language arts and mathematics. The interface between teachers from the regular and

Title I programs was smooth, and classroom teachers were pleased to have assistance in the classroom. One teacher who was

Table 5. Goals and Strategies of Madison Elementary's Title I Plan

Goals
1. Increase achievement in language arts and mathematics
2. Increase the use of computers as instructional tools
3. Provide staff development
4. Increase parent involvement

Instructional strategies
1. Computer assisted instruction
2. Literature based activities
3. Whole language
4. Cooperative learning
5. Thematic units
6. Hands-on techniques in mathematics
7. Reading Recovery
8. Higher order thinking
9. NRT/CRT results based lessons
10. Alternative assessment
11. Heterogeneous, multi-age groups
12. Inquiry approach in science
13. Team teaching/ collaborative planning

Staff development
1. Technology
2. Literature based activities
3. Whole language
4. Problem solving activities in mathematics
5. Hands on/manipulatives
6. Lesson planning using NRT/CRT scores
7. Alternative assessment techniques
8. Team teaching

Parent Involvement
1. Workshops and parent functions
2. Parent participation in planning school programs
3. Parent center and
4. Parent liaison
5. Faculty-parent meetings
6. Parent visitation in classrooms
7. Regular communications home
8. Parent volunteer program

---

interviewed commented that "Instead of two hands, there are four," and added that teaming increased the opportunities for students to get individualized attention. Another teacher explained teaming with the Title I teacher a little differently, saying during the interview, "The new thing is that we work together in the classroom cooperatively. The emphasis is on helping the kids in the classroom."

A change that occurred through the schoolwide plan, and that facilitated the success of team teaching, was time devoted to planning collaboratively. Teachers saw their weekly planning time as a distinct advantage, describing the time as a helpful forum for sharing ideas and materials. Interestingly, at Madison, collaborative planning involved not only the grade level and the Title I teachers, and ancillary professionals, but also the lead teacher at the school, and even the principal from time to time. This practice is a contrast to conditions at Lincoln where a lead teacher had also been assigned, but was not described as an active participant in the schoolwide program during the visit to the school.

Teaming was the norm at Madison; however students were also occasionally pulled out of the classroom for special instruction. Ms. Denny explained that the decision to remove a student from the regular classroom for Title I services reduced the pupil-teacher ratio. However, the decision to remove a student or group of students was made jointly by the classroom and Title I teachers. In this way, both teachers had input into activities that would take place with students who were out of the classroom as well as with those who remained in the classroom.

A major strategy at Madison for increasing reading achievement was Reading Recovery, a program designed to build reading skills in children who are non-readers or who have great difficulty learning to read. Over $80,000 was budgeted for the Reading

Recovery program. When observed, the Reading Recovery teacher worked one-on-one with a student, concluding by giving him the book to take home for practice. According to this teacher, she taught 17 students each day, pulling them from regular classes for individual or small group work. She said several Madison students had met with success and had graduated from the program.

As had occurred at Lincoln, the overall instructional program at Madison was assessed. The site visit team observed in 7 of the 14 regular classrooms, and as at Lincoln, instructional weaknesses were discovered through these observations. Thirteen instructional strategies were included in the plan, including computer-assisted instruction, literature-based activities, whole language, cooperative learning, thematic units, and hands-on activities in mathematics.

Table 6. Number of Times Each Instructional Component of the Title I Plan was Observed in Seven Classrooms at Madison Elementary

Program components	Times Observed
Computer Assisted Instruction	1
Literature literacy based activities	4
Whole Language	1
Cooperative groups	4
Thematic units	0
Hands-on techniques/ math manipulatives	0[a]
Higher order thinking	4
Alternative assessment	0
Inquiry approach in science	0

[a] Two mathematics lessons were observed.

Some strategies included in the Title I plan were observable in classrooms, as can be seen in Table 6. Most frequently observed of these strategies were activities that were literature-based, activities that used cooperative and small groups, and lessons that tapped students' higher order thinking. Each of these strategies was observed in four of the seven classes visited. Caveats exist, however. Observers noted that higher order thinking opportunities occurred occasionally rather than as an integral part of a lesson, thus there was little effect on building proficiency with these skills among the students. Similarly, the success of cooperative grouping varied, with disturbances in one class signaling that the students had not yet mastered group work. Strategies in the Title I plan that were not observed at all included thematic units, hands-on techniques, alternative assessment, and inquiry approach in science.

A strong emphasis at the school was lessons oriented toward skill-and-drill or knowledge acquisition. Six of the seven classrooms visited had this emphasis. Strong academic press was observed in only two classes where lessons were fast-paced and off-task behavior was not allowed. These teachers helped students make the connection between their learning tasks and a larger body of knowledge. These two classes were counterbalanced by two others in which academic press was weak and the teachers exhibited very low expectations for student learning, allowing off-task behavior to go uncorrected.

Results from the CET provide evidence that improvements needed to be made in instructional practices. The mean score for teachers on the instructional indicators, reported in Table 7, was 2.5. A score of 2.0 indicates that performance sometimes meets expectations, but improvement is needed to meet expectations consistently. Madison teachers scored below 2.5 on half of the instructional indicators. The highest scores were for "communicating with students" (3.1) and "presenting content at an appropriate level" (3.0). Teachers scored lowest on the indicators, "uses techniques that develop the lesson effectively" (2.1) and "encouraging higher order thinking" (2.0). The mean score on the management indicators was also 2.5. Problematic with regard to management skills were timely transitions, making time adjustments for activities that were planned, and monitoring students to facilitate their learning, for which the mean score was 2.3.

The principal and teachers completed questionnaires that included items about instructional practices. The principal at Madison agreed with the responding teachers that the faculty did a good job with instruction. However, some of the questionnaire results were not corroborated by the observational findings.

Most teachers (88%) marked that the faculty used a variety of instructional strategies, including hands-on activities, and 63% indicated that they related content to students' everyday lives. During classroom observations, as noted, no hands-on activities were observed, and strategies tended to be rote skill building assignments.

Also problematic was that increasing achievement in language arts and mathematics was an important goal of the Title I program at Madison, yet only half of the teachers felt a good job

Table 7. Madison Elementary Mean CET Scores

Indicators by Domain	Mean
Instructional Indicators	2.5
Uses techniques which develop lesson effectively	2.1
Sequences lesson to promote learning	2.3
Uses available materials to achieve lesson objectives	2.3
Adjusts lesson when appropriate	2.5
Presents content at developmentally appropriate level	3.0
Presents accurate subject matter	2.6
Relates relevant examples...or events to content	2.3
Accommodates individual differences	2.6
Communicates effectively with students	3.1
Stimulates and encourages higher order thinking	2.0
Encourages student participation	2.9
Monitors on-going performance of students	2.4
Provides feedback to students regarding their progress	2.6

Management Indicators	2.5
Organizes space, materials, equipment to facilitate learning	2.7
Promotes a positive learning climate	2.3
Manages routines/transitions in timely manner	2.4
Manages/adjusts time for planned activities	2.3

NOTE: Scores are as follows: 1=Unsatisfactory; 2=Improvement Needed; 3 = Area of Strength; 4 = Demonstrates Excellence. The midpoint is 2.5.

was done in preparing students in these areas. This perception may have been shared by the students as well. When asked whether students learn more at Madison than at other schools, only half of the students agreed. The test scores indicated that these teachers and students were accurate in their assessment.

Reasons for the low achievement at Madison may be rooted in the faculty's perceptions of the students. Questionnaire results indicated that expectations for student achievement were low. Both Ms. Denny and 71% of the teachers rated the academic ability of Madison students as lower than at other schools. On the other hand, the students disagreed, with 93% believing they could do very well academically.

In contrast to their expectations for the students, teachers had a strong sense of their own efficacy. Eighty-eight percent of the responding teachers believed that through their actions, they could insure high achievement levels. Yet only 63% agreed that the faculty could be successful with Madison students. Perhaps because the faculty had little confidence in students' ability to learn, a disturbing 38% of Madison teachers noted that students were encouraged to do extra work to improve their grades.

Increase the use of computers as instructional tools. Madison received slightly more than $15,000 in Title I funds for equipping a computer lab. However, the expenditure seemed to have little impact on overall computer literacy or the integration of technology into the instructional program. The lab was equipped with 12 computers, but during an observation of lab activities, 10 students shared four computers to complete practice and drill activities in mathematics and reading.

Other observational data showed that computers in classrooms were seldom used. Observers in seven classes recorded a computer in use only one time. Despite a desire expressed by Ms. Denny to improve students' computer literacy, it did not appear to be occurring at the school. Failure to follow through with staff development may have been the culprit. Five of the teachers who were interviewed said that lack of staff development was an impediment to their use of the computers.

<u>Provide staff development.</u> Over a two-year period, Title I funding for staff development amounted to a small $2,800, according to a budget analysis. Both Ms. Denny and the teachers who were interviewed said that staff development was a regular activity at Madison. Teachers described monthly meetings that occurred on days when students were dismissed early to provide time for staff development. During these sessions, discussions occurred about the instructional program and the school improvement plan. In addition, other forms of staff development included previously mentioned weekly grade level meetings; demonstration lessons taught by Ms. Denny and/or the lead teacher; and feedback to the faculty from teachers involved in off-campus training.

According to Ms. Denny, specific issues addressed through staff development were early literacy, grouping strategies for reading, and ways to involve parents in students' reading and provide them with feedback about students' progress. Interestingly, she did not mention computer training. Teachers who were interviewed mentioned a number of staff development activities including literature-based teaching, whole language, hands-on techniques, diversity, multi-age grouping, using an inquiry approach in science, and writing instruction. As discussed above, only a few of these activities were observed in classroom.

The lack of transfer into practice prompted some doubt about the effectiveness of the Madison staff development program. Survey results provided a mixed picture. Approximately three-fourths of the teachers at Madison felt that staff development addressed important issues and developed skills to enhance teaching. A similar number also agreed that the faculty helped determine staff development activities. However, only 26% of teachers rated the activities of high quality in comparison to other schools. These data suggest that not only the quantity, but also the quality, of staff development must be considered if Title I school-wide programs are to result in differences in schools.

Increase parental involvement. Ms. Denny described efforts to promote parent involvement in students' learning and at the school. She said that each grade level held parent meetings which were typically attended by approximately 20 parents. She noted that parents volunteered at the school, performed clerical chores, and chaperoned field trips. Members of the site visit team noted that parent volunteers were observed in three of the seven class-rooms visited.

Teacher views were mixed regarding parent involvement. Four of the eight teachers who were interviewed commented that parents were reasonably involved, and five said that parents responded well to phone calls. However, only one-fourth of the teachers responding to the questionnaire indicated that they thought parents were involved sufficiently in school activities. Reasons for the discrepancy were not discovered. In contrast to Lincoln, where few teachers thought parents cared about grades, at Madison 76% of the teachers thought parents cared about their children's grades. The researchers speculate again that teachers' belief about parents' interest in their child is connected to how well the teachers knew the parents. At Madison, 75% of the teachers, compared to 57% of the teachers at Lincoln, knew the parent of most of their students.

Principal's Leadership

Ms. Denny was in her twenty-fourth year as an educator, and Madison teachers found her very involved in instruction and supportive of instructional efforts. For example, she often participated in grade-level planning meetings. Enthusiastic about improving Madison, she stated her pride in the school and mentioned that since her arrival on campus, a Student of the Month program was implemented to honor a student "not neces-sarily for being an 'A' or 'B' student but for being a good citizen." She also stated that a personal goal of hers was to bring computer literacy to students and to teachers who, she felt, were often reluctant to use computers. Unfortunately, this personal goal appeared to be unmet.

Unlike the Lincoln principal, Ms. Denny had a strong sense of personal efficacy, believing her efforts were vital to ensuring that all Madison students achieved at a high level. Her proactive leadership style and can-do attitude about the school gave a positive message. Despite having no input in the Title I plan that was operational during her first year as principal, Ms. Denny actively worked to make things better at Madison and looked forward to addressing school needs with a modified plan for subsequent years. By teaching demonstration lessons for the faculty, she made instruction a priority, signaling to the entire school community the importance of teaching and learning. Ms. Denny believed that with teacher cooperation, Madison could become a high-achieving school, and she encouraged teacher involvement in school improvement planning.

Teacher perceptions about Ms. Denny's leadership style were positive. A majority of teachers indicated she encouraged their involvement in decision-making (88%) and in the school improve-ment process (88%). Like Lincoln teachers, most Madison teachers gave the principal high marks for protecting instructional time (76%). Further, most Madison teachers considered Ms. Denny to be supportive of their efforts to improve achievement (75%), visible at school (75%), and actively engaged in providing resources for the school (100%).

School Climate

Unlike Lincoln, where the principal and teachers differed in their perceptions of school safety, Ms. Denny and a majority of the teachers agreed that Madison was a safe place for both students and staff (88%). Additionally, most Madison teachers indicated they were supported in disciplinary matters (88%), with consistent enforcement of discipline policy by administration.

Madison students indicated the school was safe (86%), but not orderly. Classes were frequently interrupted by disruptive children, in the opinion of 87% of the responding students. Nonetheless, students had positive perceptions of instruction and teachers. Ninety-eight percent of the students indicated that teachers taught them things they needed to know and 85% agreed that teachers graded them fairly. According to the students, teachers communicated that learning was important, with 95% of the students indicating that this was the case. Likewise, 90% of the students said that teachers helped students who did poorly.

Just as their counterparts at Lincoln had done when asked to name the three best things about school, most Madison students selected teachers, with 29 students naming teachers as one of the three best things about the school. Students commented that teachers were caring and nice, taught "in a way that we can understand it, and "best of all, the teachers always keep us from getting into trouble." A more distant second than occurred at Lincoln, 20 Madison students said they liked breaks from class, such as recess and lunch. Finally, 15 students wrote that being with "friends" and "nice people" was one of the best things about school.

Also consistent with the choice of Lincoln students, 23 students at Madison named disobedient and "mean" students as one of the worst things about the school. Specific student comments included, "People talk back and sometimes curse, and I don't like that," and "Some people tease me." Mentioned second most often as one of the worst things at Madison was the physical condition of the school, with 22 students noting conditions as a problem. Showing an awareness of the poor physical state of the school, students wrote "We have holes in the roof and water comes through," and "We need paint jobs." Finally, 17 students named student fights as a negative aspect of the school. Unlike Lincoln students who named specific subjects as among the worst things about school, Madison students seemed much more pleased with the learning activities in which they participated.

Of the many ways that school climate manifests itself, one of the most telling is job satisfaction. At Madison, the principal and teachers indicated that job satisfaction was high. Questionnaire results showed Ms. Denny and most teachers looked forward to coming to work (88%), and would choose to stay at the school if offered a transfer (75%). By contrast, almost half of the faculty at Lincoln indicated they would prefer to transfer from the school.

Summary of Madison Elementary

Madison Elementary School made some progress toward realizing its Title I goals. Some of the instructional strategies were being implemented, staff development had been provided, and there was evidence that parent involvement was improving. A new principal had infused her enthusiasm into many of the faculty and exhibited genuine instructional leadership, teaching demonstration lessons and meeting with teachers during grade level meetings. Yet, students at Madison continued to struggle on the NRT and CRT assessments administered by the district.

It is possible to speculate about the causes for the lackluster student achievement. Ms. Denny arrived at the school as a first-year principal. She replaced a retiring principal who had led the school for 20 years, and under whose leadership little headway was made toward change or innovation. A complicated Title I schoolwide plan confronted Ms. Denny on her arrival. Despite her enthusiasm, the multiple instructional strategies included in the plan and addressed through staff development did not transfer into classroom implementation. It seems probable that the faculty's low expectations for student achievement may have contributed to a sense that different teaching strategies were unlikely to overcome the deficits the children were perceived to have, making the difficulty of changing practice not a worthwhile investment. This combination of circumstances overpowered the principal's efforts to improve the school, and the teaching at Madison remained as lackluster as the test scores.

Discussion

The purpose of our study was to examine why the Title I schoolwide programs at the two schools garnered such poor results. Despite funding for additional personnel, materials, and staff development, the schoolwide programs at both Lincoln Elementary and Madison Elementary were ineffective. Several contributors to this ineffectiveness were common to Lincoln and Madison. First, Title I plans laid out strategies that were too numerous to be effectively implemented. There was no attempt to scaffold the plans so that strategies implemented in one year provided a foundation for the following year. A more narrow focus with a sequential plan for implementation was needed. Second, technology was not being utilized to augment the instructional program. Both schools included computer usage as a goal of the schoolwide program. At Lincoln the principal was openly hostile to computers, while at Madison the principal named increased computer literacy among staff and students as a personal goal. Given these differences in the orientation of the two principals, it was a surprise to find that the integration of computers into the instructional program was actually greater at Lincoln. At neither school, however, were computers viewed by the faculty as an integral tool for achieving other instructional goals.

A third contributor to the ineffectiveness of the schoolwide programs was poor instruction. Low confidence in student ability led teachers to present a minimalist curriculum strongly devoted to skill building and drill activities at the expense of nurturing students' higher order thinking skills through thematic units, use of the Internet, or other methods. This problem is linked to the fourth contributor, poor classroom management skills. Teachers' lack of respect for carefully using students' time and/or their own inability to manage the students led to much wasted instructional time. It is possible that scores at both schools could increase if the wasted time in the classroom were redirected.

In spite of these common dilemmas, leadership is the variable on which a more optimistic future for Madison can be hinged. As an agent of change, the principal often sets the tone for a school, by helping to shape the way teaching and learning are viewed. At Madison, Ms. Denny's administrative style and strong sense of efficacy offered hope for positive change. Although her tenure in the position was short, Ms. Denny proved to be a strong principal, involved in dual roles as instructional leader and school manager. Evidence of Ms. Denny's commitment to excellence and responsibility toward students was found in her willingness to teach demonstration lessons for teachers, which strengthened the connection between her and the faculty. She was able to harness teacher energies in the direction of school improvement by encouraging collaboration. Madison teachers indicated they felt they were part of a team effort to improve the school's instructional program.

On the other hand, Ms. Carson's administrative style had a negative impact on the culture of Lincoln Elementary. An ineffective instructional leader, she held low expectations for student learning, and low performance followed. After ten plus years as the principal, she viewed her impact on student achievement as marginal, indicating there was little probability of increasing student achievement while she remained principal of the school. Her low sense of efficacy permeated the academic climate at Lincoln, prompting over half of the teachers to indicate that if given a chance, they would at least consider, if not accept, a transfer to another school.

As shown in this chapter, the receipt of Title I funding did not guarantee success for Lincoln and Madison Elementary Schools. To be successful, a school needs an organized plan for effectively using resources. This requires a visionary and proactive leader capable of identifying the various strengths and weaknesses within the school, developing a plan responsive to those strengths and weaknesses, and galvanizing the school community into action.

References

McCoy, M. H. & Taylor, D. L. (2000, April). Does Block Scheduling Live Up to its Promise? Paper presented at the annual meeting of the American Educational Research Association, New Orleans, Louisiana.

Taylor, D. L., Ratcliff, E. & Kemper, E. A. (1999, January). Effects of District Level Decisions on Title I Schoolwide Programs at the Secondary Level. Paper presented at the annual meeting of the Southwest Educational Research Association, San Antonio, Texas.

Taylor, D. L. and Teddlie, C. B. (1999). Implementation Fidelity in Title I Schoolwide Programs. *Journal of Education for Students Placed at Risk, 4,* 229-319.

SECTION III.

Lessons Learned From the Field

CHAPTER 8

COMPREHENSIVE SCHOOL REFORM: LESSONS LEARNED

James Meza, Jr., Lesley Dahlkemper, & Joan Buttram

Introduction

In November 1997, the United States Congress created the Comprehensive School Reform Demonstration (CSRD) program, which provides financial incentives for schools, particularly Title I schools, to support the implementation of schoolwide, research-based initiatives to raise achievement for all students. Traditionally, federal dollars have been targeted for individual programs. Keltner (1998) states that traditional school efforts have focused on improving specific and isolated achievement deficits. For example, a school may adopt a whole language or phonics program to address reading problems while another school may introduce a new math series to address a math problem. This patchwork approach to reform is what he describes as the "Christmas Tree Effect" to school improvement.

CSRD which is a result of bi-partisan legislation, sponsored by Representatives John Porter (Republican from Illinois) and David Obey (Democrat from Wisconsin), is a dramatically different approach to school reform and focuses on reorganizing and revitalizing the entire school rather than on isolated, piecemeal, or fragmented approaches to reform. What distinguishes this legislation is its clear message that a collection of such add-on programs do not necessarily affect school reform; comprehensive reform takes into account what educators have learned in earlier reform efforts (Cincchinelli, 1999).

CSRD is a school improvement strategy that uses best practices, and researched and well-documented school reform models. This legislation mentions examples of comprehensive reform models, such as Accelerated Schools, ATLAS Communities, Audrey Cohen College, Coalition of Essential Schools, Community for Learning, Co-NECT, Direct Instruction, Expeditionary Learning, Outward Bound, High Schools That Work, Modern Little Red School House, National Alliance for Restructuring Education, Paideia, Roots and Wings, School Development Program, Success For All, Talent Development High School, and Urban Learning Center. The law also allows schools to create their own comprehensive reforms – so called "homegrown" or locally developed models – as long as they meet the CSRD criteria. The ultimate goal of CSRD is to enable all children in the schools served, particularly low-achieving children, to meet challenging state content and student performance standards.

Criteria for CSRD

More specifically, a comprehensive school reform program is defined by the congressional legislation as one that integrates in a coherent manner, all nine of the following components (Education Commission of the States, 1998):

- *Effective, research based methods and strategies:* A comprehensive school reform program employs innovative strategies and proven methods for student learning, teaching, and school management that are based on reliable and effective practices, and have been replicated successfully in schools with diverse characteristics.
- *Comprehensive design with aligned components:* The program has a comprehensive design for effective school functioning (including instruction, assessment, classroom management, professional development, parental involvement, and school management) that aligns the school's curriculum, technology, and professional development into a school reform plan designed to enable all students – including children from low-income families, children with limited English proficiency, and children with disabilities – to meet challenging state content and performance standards and addresses needs identified through a school needs assessment.

- *Professional development:* The program provides high-quality and continuous teacher and staff professional development and training.
- *Measurable goals and benchmarks:* A comprehensive school reform program has measurable goals for students' performance tied to the state's challenging content and student performance standards, as those standards are implemented, and benchmarks for meeting the goals.
- *Support within the school:* The program is supported by school faculty, administrators, and staff.
- *Parental and community involvement:* The program provides for the meaningful involvement of parents and the local community in planning and implementing school improvement activities.
- *External technical support and assistance*: A comprehensive reform program utilizes high-quality external support and assistance from a comprehensive school reform entity (which may be a university) with experience or expertise in school reform and improvement.
- *Evaluation strategies:* The program includes a plan for an evaluation of the implementation of a school's reform and the student results achieved.
- *Coordination of resources:* The program identifies how other resources (Federal, State, local, and private) available to the school will be utilized to coordinate services to support and sustain the school reform.

The Congressional Conference Report on CSRD specifies that reform models must employ proven methods for student learning, have been replicated successfully in other schools, and provide high-quality professional development for teachers.

Funding

During fiscal year 1998, $145 million was available to state education agencies to provide incentive grants to school districts on a competitive basis, for schools that elect to pursue comprehensive school reforms. Funding of $120 million was available under the Title I Demonstrations of Innovative Practices Program and $25 million was available under the Fund for the Improvement of Education (FIE). Title I funds are allocated to state educational agencies (SEA) based on the Title I basic grant formula, and FIE funds are allocated to SEAs based on each state's relative share of the school-age population. CSRD provides for approximately 3,000 schools to receive grants of not less than $50,000, renewable for two years. The actual number of schools participating would depend on the cost of the particular reform model chosen or designed by each school.

CSRD funds alone are not intended to support the full implementation of a comprehensive reform program on an ongoing basis. The CSRD legislation and other education improvement initiatives, such as Title I schoolwide programs, Goals 2000, and School to Work, are designed to support, in a coordinated fashion, comprehensive education improvement strategies to enable all children to reach challenging academic standards. A school engaged in comprehensive school reform is expected to coordinate all of the resources available to it, including federal, state, and private funding.

Developing Applications and Guidelines for States and School Districts

The U.S. Department of Education (USDE) is charged with developing the application process and distributing federal comprehensive school reform funding to SEAs. All 50 states have applied for and are receiving funding which the USDE began distributing in fiscal year 1998. As the USDE approved state funding, states had to demonstrate in their applications:

- *Selection criteria:* The state's application must describe the process and the criteria the SEA will use to make competitive grants to districts, including any competitive preferences it establishes.
- *Strategies to ensure quality:* The SEA must explain how it will ensure the adoption of only high-quality and well-documented comprehensive school reform programs integrating the nine criteria established in the federal legislation.
- *Dissemination strategies:* The SEA must describe how it will work with other partners, including the Regional Education Laboratories and the Comprehensive Regional Assistance Centers, to disseminate materials identifying research based comprehensive school reform models. SEAs must show how its staff, with support from partners,

will provide technical assistance to assist districts and schools in evaluating, selecting, and implementing comprehensive school reforms.

- *State evaluation strategies:* Each state's application must describe how the SEA will measure the results in improved student performance and evaluate the implementation of comprehensive school reforms funded by the USDE.

Under the CSRD legislation, an SEA may set aside up to five percent of its CSRD funding for administrative, evaluation, and technical assistance expenses, including expenses necessary to inform districts and schools about research based comprehensive school reform approaches. The remaining funds must be earmarked for competitive grants to eligible districts.

As the USDE approved states for funding under the CSRD project, states faced the hard work of reviewing applications submitted by districts and schools seeking funding to implement schoolwide reform. As SEAs awarded funding to districts on a competitive basis, they targeted funding at schools with the greatest need for reform. Heavy emphasis is placed on low performing Title I schools, which underscores the intent of the legislation to foster change in schools that have continually failed to increase student achievement. In addition to focusing on geographical diversity and varying grade levels, middle and high schools with high drop-out rates, or schools that are feeders for these schools, were also targeted.

In addition to these factors, SEAs are encouraged to give preference to schools implementing effective, research based comprehensive reform programs that cover all aspects of their operations, rather than approving funds for schools that simply add on programs to existing reform efforts. Locally developed programs, as long as they meet the nine criteria, are eligible for funds as well.

Under CSRD, the emphasis is on ongoing, high quality, external support and assistance from a comprehensive school reform entity with expertise in schoolwide reform. As SEA staff reviewed applications from districts and schools, they took a hard look at the type of assistance schools would receive, based on the belief that comprehensive school reform's success will largely be determined by the quality of the technical assistance to schools. Universities, comprehensive school reform model developers, the

Regional Educational Laboratories, Comprehensive Regional Assistance Centers, or other external entities can provide this assistance. The USDE expected support not only during the early implementation phases of a reform model, but throughout the implementation of the school's comprehensive reform program.

Finally, districts and schools applying for CSRD funding from the state were also required to establish which schools would receive CSRD funding and how much; describe which models would be adopted; explain in detail how the school district would support comprehensive school reform efforts, including what additional resources would be committed to the effort (e.g., federal, state, local and private funding); and how the district would evaluate whether the reform model was improving student achievement.

First Year Implementation

A key feature of CSRD was the flexibility provided to states for developing and submitting their respective plans. According to information provided by the Southwest Educational Development Lab (SEDL), states were able to submit their plans over approximately a 15-month period, beginning in the early spring of 1998 and ending in the early summer of 1999. This timeline suggests that states took advantage of the flexibility to consider how best to integrate CSRD funding with their own reform efforts. States that submitted their plans later were able to learn important lessons from the states that initiated their CSRD programs early on. Although a few states, such as Kansas, Maryland, Illinois, and Wisconsin, moved extremely quickly to award their CSRD funds, many states chose to delay their competitions until the fall of 1998 to allow local education agencies (LEAs) sufficient time to complete or update needs assessments, investigate different comprehensive school reform models and form relationships with particular developers, and prepare plans for their proposed efforts. In hindsight, some of the states who jump-started their programs wished they had gone slower, and some who delayed their initial competitions until the fall wished they had allowed even more time for local planning.

As noted above, all 50 states have made CSRD awards (SEDL, 1999). Multiple competitions were held in approximately one-third of the states. In some states, insufficient numbers of high quality proposals were submitted in the first round, and additional rounds were necessary in order to spend all of the funding. In other states, the SEA divided the pool of funds and conducted two or more rounds to allow those LEAs that were ready to get started as soon as possible and those that needed more planning time to compete at a later date. Allowing individual states the flexibility to decide when to schedule their competitions and how many competitions to hold is a major strength of this program.

The legislative language required that a minimum of $50,000 be awarded to an individual school building. If the minimum were awarded in all cases, approximately 2,755 schools would receive funding. However, since some states awarded more than the minimum amount the total number of schools is less. As of November 1999, the 50 states, Puerto Rico, and the Bureau of Indian Affairs have reported funding a total of 1,753 awards (SEDL, 1999).

The United States Congress Conference Report on CSRD (U.S. Department of Education, 1998) divided the funds into two pools, Title I eligible and FIE. Only schools that were eligible for Title I funds could apply for funding through the first pool; any school could apply for the second. States were also allowed to target their funding by adding other criteria, and some states elected to direct funding to particular grade levels, to schools that had failed to meet particular student achievement or performance standards, or some other criteria.

The majority of the first year funding has been distributed to Title 1 schools (86.0%). Three-fourths (74.5%) of the awards have gone to schools with Title I schoolwide programs, 17.0 percent to Title I schools with targeted assistance, and almost half (48.1%) to schools targeted for ESEA improvement. Almost two-thirds of the awards have been made to elementary schools (65.9%), another fifth to middle schools (20.2%), and the remainder to secondary schools (13.9%). These percentages are consistent with usual the distribution of Title I funds; each year the majority goes to elementary schools.

The CSRD awards are distributed to schools across the country. Approximately 70% of the awards were given to schools in either large central or mid-sized cities or the urban fringes surrounding these cities. Another 12% went to small and large towns. The remaining 18% went to rural schools.

At the start of the CSRD program, there was significant discussion as to whether the federal or state governments ought to limit the eligibility of models to ensure that only research based models or models that matched state priorities or standards would be selected by local education agencies (LEAs). The federal government decided not to limit the eligibility of particular models, opting instead to establish criteria that any model must meet. In most cases, the SEAs followed the USDE's lead and did not limit the choice of LEAs, instead requiring applicants to document that the selected comprehensive school reform model met the established criteria. The SEDL database currently lists 278 models adopted by individual LEAs, significantly more than the 17 comprehensive school reform models listed in the original legislation (SEDL, 1999). Slightly over half of the awards are accounted for by eleven CSR models, and of these eleven, eight were mentioned in the original conference language. Two resource documents, one prepared by the regional educational labs under the leadership of the Northwest Regional Educational Laboratory and the other prepared by the American Institutes for Research, suggest that many of the adopted models fall short in meeting these criteria.

Lessons Learned

Comprehensive reform pushed schoolwide educational reform into the national spotlight. For the first time, Congress, the USDE, state legislatures, SEAs, school districts, and schools are required to examine how they structure school improvement programs, how public accountability fits in, and how best to provide support to schools. CSRD has placed new challenges and expectations for educational leaders which include: integrating comprehensive school reform into broader reform efforts at the state, district, and local levels; ensuring in-depth and quality technical assistance from developers, some of whom are already stretched thin by high demand; and providing timely information that assists state and district leaders in becoming savvy consumers of research based designs and other models that claim to be comprehensive in scope.

CSRD requires work and commitment from federal policymakers, state education departments, state legislators, district administrators, and school faculty. These roles, and the lessons learned from USDOE, states, districts, and schools that have successfully implemented comprehensive reform, are described in more detail next.

Federal Level

Flexible State Timeline and Peer Review Process

The federal government's decisions to use a flexible roll-out period (i.e., SEAs could decide when to submit their plan and hold individual state level competitions) and rely on a peer review process were critical in helping this program to move forward successfully (W. Kincaid, personal communication, November 22, 1999). States that were able to develop their plans and proceed quickly could do so, and other states that needed more time were not penalized and forced to proceed prematurely. This luxury of time provided states with breathing room to consider fully how best to use their funding and to insert the CSRD competition into their own reform agenda and timeline in a coherent way.

The peer review process itself provided numerous benefits. First, it allowed USDE staff to include SEA representatives in the review process and benefit from their expertise in designing statewide comprehensive reform efforts. Second, through participation in the panels, peer reviewers from the SEAs were able to learn more about comprehensive school reform as well as successful (and unsuccessful) strategies. Third, federal CSRD staff were able to build stronger connections with SEA staff; these relationships will serve both levels well as the demonstration program unfolds over time.

Guidance for the CSRD Program

Another key feature of this initiative was the Guidance for the Comprehensive School Reform Demonstration program provided by the federal department (U.S. Department of Education, 1998). Through a series of questions and answers, this Guidance addressed the purpose of the CSRD program, components of a comprehensive school reform program, federal awards to states, state application requirements, funds reserved for state use, state awards to LEAs, local use of funds, technical assistance, and evaluation. Unlike regulatory language written for many federal initiatives, the Guidance helped both SEA and LEA staff think differently about CSRD funds, to see more clearly how these funds could be used to reinforce existing state reform efforts and sound school improvement practices.

Framework for Assessing the Research Base and Effectiveness of CSR Models

The USDE elected to establish criteria to help assess whether a particular comprehensive school reform model should be adopted as part of the CSRD program (U.S. Department of Education, 1998). The criteria were organized into a framework with four dimensions: (a) theoretical or research findings that explain why a comprehensive school reform model and the practices included in the model work together to produce gains in student performance, (b) evidence that educationally significant improvements in student achievement in major subject areas occurred as a result of model implementation, (c) a description of what is required to make the model fully operational, and (d) evidence that the model has been successfully implemented in more than one school (or replicability). The framework also proposed a series of questions to help potential applicants decide whether the evidence was most rigorous, somewhat rigorous, or marginal.

The framework and questions helped many states and potential applicants assess and compare CSR models and the likelihood that particular models would produce similar results in a particular school. This framework was invaluable in clarifying or operationalizing what the U.S. Congress and the USDE had in mind in terms of research based models that have proven track records of promoting educationally significant improvements in student achievement. Subsequent federal initiatives have incorporated this framework into their requirements as well.

National Database on CSRD Awards

Almost by chance, a database was created to track CSRD awards. One of the ten regional educational laboratories, the Southwest Educational Development Laboratory (SEDL), had offered to create a national database of awardees as part of its ongoing assistance to support the CSRD program. The original intent of the database was to help the ten regional educational laboratories create networks of funded programs primarily for communication, training, and research purposes. When USDE officials heard about this proposal, they asked if the database could be expanded to serve the purpose of reporting awards by state, along with basic descriptive data on each award. SEDL quickly agreed to this suggestion, and the CSRD Awardee Database was born (SEDL, 1998).

The database consists of both public and restricted information data files. The public data file contains basic school and district contact and descriptive information about each award, such as the comprehensive school reform model selected, Title I status, geographic locale, grade levels, and amount and length of award. The restricted data file is available to USDE staff and includes more sensitive descriptive information.

The existence of such a database is highly unusual; previous USDE initiatives have not had either public or restricted databases. The database has been used by Congressional staff and federal and state officials to chart and describe the rollout of the CSRD program. It also has been used by researchers to help construct samples and collect other descriptive data about CSRD awards (K. Doherty, personal communication, November 23, 1999).

Evaluations at All Levels

This federal initiative has generated a flurry of research and evaluation studies at the state, local, and national levels. The federal government requires SEAs and LEAs to examine both implementation and outcome data, thus potentially generating over 2,000 evaluations (U.S. Department of Education, 1998). In addition, researchers from many of the regional educational laboratories, universities, and other R&D organizations have proposed their own evaluation and research studies. Keeping track of the multitude of studies, much less making sense of all of the findings, will present a major challenge to the federal government and other parties who have a stake in learning from this demonstration program.

To date, the majority of these studies seem to focus on documenting the progress of CSRD schools at very global levels, studying how implementation plays out in different contexts or for different populations of students, examining the extent to which the nine components are implemented in schools, how they are implemented, and tracking student outcomes. As a result, many of these studies will replicate what we already know about how difficult it is to make meaningful and lasting school improvement. Few of the studies have been designed to deepen our understanding about how to make and support meaningful changes in classroom instruction that significantly improve student performance, the heart of the problem facing Title I or low performing schools (Buttram, 1999). Until evaluations are focused on such issues, the promise that CSRD will make a significant contribution in improving the performance of Title I schools will remain unfulfilled.

A second missing evaluation perspective focuses on the critical components or features of CSR models. This is especially the case at the federal and state levels where opportunities potentially exist to look systematically across models. Because of the federal emphasis on implementation and student outcomes, few of the evaluations have been designed to gather information on the comparative success of different models, or features of models that are more closely linked to improved student outcomes. Given the large number of models being implemented across the country, it seems highly likely that some common set of components or features exist. In order to understand what these critical features are, comparisons of different models, or components of such models, could be very helpful in deepening our understanding of the necessary components. Adding such comparisons to proposed evaluations could be very helpful.

State Level

Making State Dollars Work Smarter for Education Reform

Implementing good comprehensive school reform models costs money. Keltner (1998) indicates that although the Obey-Porter legislation provides a boost to comprehensive reform, the funding level per school may not be sufficient. Keltner found that although design services are on average estimated at $25,000, this is about 16% of the total implementation costs. Other resources that need to be considered are personnel allocation to support the design, new instructional materials and professional conferences, and teacher release time. Overall, the average resource use for comprehensive reform is close to $180,000 per school site.

To meet these and other costs tied to schoolwide reform, states are thinking harder about pooling increasingly tight resources for greatest impact. Just as schools must be clear about their goals for improving student achievement, comprehensive school reform is leading many state level education leaders to focus on bringing all of their resources to bear on improving schools. By combining federal comprehensive school reform funds with Goals 2000 money, Title I dollars, and other state revenue earmarked for low-performing schools, state leaders say they are better at targeting dollars where most needed. Experts agree that deciding how best to allocate funds is one of the most powerful ways to help comprehensive school reform take root. There is now added incentive, as some policy makers push for the entire federal Title I program, literally billions of dollars, to focus exclusively on comprehensive school reform.

States are using varying methods of coordination resources to support comprehensive reform. Wisconsin assembled state leaders of funding programs such as Title I, Special Education, and Goals 2000. Together, they created training programs for school and district leaders on how to direct these funding sources toward comprehensive school reform. In Florida, the state listed all of the state and federal grants that could be used to help pay for comprehensive reform efforts and shared the list with districts and schools. California, Florida, Illinois, Maryland, and New York required schools applying for federal comprehensive school reform funds to explain, in detail, how the school and district will use all of their financial and personnel resources to support the effort. The Illinois Department of Education is developing plans to use Goals 2000 Leadership money to support additional schools not funded by federal grants for comprehensive school reform. In order for comprehensive school reform to take root and flourish, experience shows several funding streams are necessary to support this effort for the long haul. Short-term investments typically fail to produce results.

Legislative Leadership

In comprehensive school reform, as in many ambitious undertakings, lessons learned from states that have effectively implemented this reform strategy show real change has taken place where leaders have challenged the status quo. Elected officials have sounded the call for change by unmasking failures in the education system and offering solutions, such as comprehensive school reform. By challenging conventional thinking, these leaders have begun to move the dialogue about how to reform schools to a new level. When difficult but necessary education reform does take hold, improved test results and a track record of success discourage people from returning to the way things were before.

Some legislators and other state policymakers have played a significant role in providing leadership that sets the tone for change and establishes comprehensive school reform as a strategy for overhauling low-performing schools by:

- Building coalitions to support reform efforts.
- Creating waivers to allow districts and schools to make policy changes to implement comprehensive reform (for example, increased time for staff development).
- Requiring that comprehensive reform efforts include the nine components mentioned in the federal legislation.
- Allocating funding, when appropriate, to support thoughtful comprehensive reform efforts.

Comprehensive school reform advocates indicate that state legislators can create the right conditions to help school reforms flourish by eliminating cumbersome regulations and providing leadership to schools and districts. Schools and districts need time to investigate programs that are effective and a good match with both local needs and state standards. When the process is rushed due to political pressures or funding deadlines, quality of implementation suffers. Legislators can make sure there is enough flexibility in the system so that schools, and students, can choose what best fits their needs. Legislators in some states have used funding allocation to encourage the use of diverse models that will meet the needs of all the students in the system, not just specific students.

State policymakers are ideally positioned to require and fund an evaluation of whether comprehensive school reform is, in fact, bolstering student performance. State standards and assessments can be used to determine how well the reforms have worked and, if not, how they can be improved in the coming years. Also, the state's accountability system comes into play, rewarding schools that have done well with more funding or freedom from regulation, and helping those that have not done well find ways to improve.

The Increasingly Important Role of State Education Departments
Federal funding for comprehensive school reform is funneled first to SEAs before it reaches districts and schools. Consequently, state departments of education staff are on the front lines of

shaping how states can assist teachers, parents, and district administrators in implementing comprehensive school reform for the long haul. In the last two years, an increasing number of SEAs are using comprehensive school reform to further their states' goals on accountability, standards, and assessments. SEAs are developing long-term strategies to help schools implement comprehensive reform and are assisting districts and schools in identifying federal, state, and district funding to support comprehensive reform. The states are also providing guidance and information to schools in choosing comprehensive reform models that match their needs.

One of the most challenging aspects of this work is examining whether schools in need are the schools that can successfully implement comprehensive school reform. In the rush to award comprehensive school reform funding to low-performing schools, some states have neglected to assess their schools' capacity for undertaking the difficult and lengthy reform process. "Often, schools that are least able to undertake reform—ones that lack leadership, structure, a supportive culture, that are dysfunctional and chaotic—are the ones most eligible to receive federal comprehensive school reform funds," says Jane Heibt, the director of planning for Expeditionary Learning/Outward Bound.

In response, some states have created special programs to help low-performing schools prepare for reform. Florida is a good example. The state department of education has created a 25 member School Improvement Staff assigned to work one-on-one with low-performing schools to craft improvement plans. The state Department of Education, SEDL, the Comprehensive Assistance Center, and Title I regional offices are collaborating to offer ongoing training and support services to schools, including a three-day leadership conference for principals and key stakeholders in schools that receive CSRD funding.

Finding the Best Match
Another challenge is ensuring a good fit between a school and a reform model, critical in creating lasting schoolwide reform efforts. Increasingly, state leaders are helping schools and districts sort through the bewildering array of information about models to make careful, informed decisions. The task is not a simple one. Not only is the sheer amount of information tough to analyze, but it is a struggle for most schools and districts, and many states, to

assess whether research presented by developers is valid. Some states, driven in part by state education agency staff, have taken steps to assist schools, including: evaluating models to make sure they are compatible with state standards; analyzing the research and guiding schools toward models that work well under a variety of social, demographic, and geographic conditions; encouraging school teams to visit schools implementing a model they are considering; and/or bringing in practitioners to talk to school staff about their experiences with a model and its developer and conducting workshops to determine whether a school and model are compatible.

An example of a structured school/design match process is used by the Accelerated Schools Project (ASP). ASP has a multi-phase school exploration and buy-in process. School communities explore the accelerated schools philosophy and process for approximately one to three months before making an informed decision to apply to become part of ASP. In order to ensure that potential schools are adequately prepared before applying, ASP prospective schools must complete all phases of the exploration and buy-in process. Exploration consists of two parts: (a) full staff (administrators, teachers, para-professionals, support staff) and parent representatives carefully studying material on ASP; and (b) after researching ASP, the school organizes a series of meetings with all members of the school community to discuss their understanding of ASP, to voice concerns, and to address questions. Ideally, school staff members invite key district personnel and school board members to join in this exploration. Buy-in consists of four parts:

1. Following the initial exploration phase, members of the school community call and/or visit existing accelerated schools to clarify any questions or concerns participants have about ASP.
2. The school community may invite someone from an existing accelerated school or a regional center to visit the school and provide an in-depth presentation and question-and-answer session.
3. Meanwhile the school community should be in the process of considering individuals, preferably from the district, who are willing to serve as prospective coaches.
4. After thoroughly exploring and researching ASP, members of the school community formally decide to embrace ASP

by taking a formal vote or coming to consensus. While a unanimous vote/consensus is optimal, a school will not be accepted without at least 90 percent of full-time staff and school community representatives willing to transform their school into an accelerated school (Levin, 1995).

Create Stability in Schools in Spite of Administrative Changes

One of the threats to successful comprehensive reform is the revolving door of leadership. Administrative turnover – at the school or district level – means that support for a program evaporates as the new principal or superintendent imposes his or her vision. Consequently, funding and attention are diverted to other programs, teachers become demoralized by seeing their hard work unravel, and the reform process grinds to a halt. With thousands of superintendent and principal positions open in this country, it is inevitable that most communities will be affected by this problem. The following are recommendations for promoting staff resilience in the midst of implementing schoolwide reform.

- *Reform networks.* Many states, districts, and developers encourage the development of reform networks made up of teachers, administrators, and others involved in implementing comprehensive reform. Through phone calls, electronic mail, training, and newsletters, staff can maintain daily contact and share innovations and teaching strategies with others in the state, region, or country.
- *Clustering.* When several schools in a district or nearby districts share the same model or "cluster," support from the developer and implementation of the model tend to be stronger. To encourage district change, states may choose to concentrate funds on schools and districts that cluster rather than those that choose a variety of models.
- *Business leaders* – Businesses have a huge stake in the success of school reform. Their future workforce is being educated in public schools. Some states, schools, and districts involve business leaders in reform efforts early, based on the belief that when a new principal or superintendent comes on board, there is more pressure to adopt the comprehensive school reform already in place. One success story is in Utah, where a group of business leaders has formed the Education Reform Foundation to support comprehensive school reform in public schools. The

group, which wants to remain anonymous, has invested up to $25,000 a year in schools that were not eligible to receive federal grants for comprehensive school reform. It works closely with the Utah Department of Education in selecting grant recipients.[1]

District and School Level

Current research on educational reform and the school district suggests that cultural changes at the school site are threatened unless the reform effort receives strong cooperation from schools and districts, including resources, investments, and a sustained focus on comprehensive reform efforts. Bodilly (1998) indicates that comprehensive reform designs with high levels of implementation were associated with districts and schools that (a) had stable leadership supportive of the effort, that lacked political crisis, (b) had a culture of trust between the central office and the schools, (c) provided some school-level autonomy, and (d) provided resources for professional development and planning.

Levin (1993) states that districts can increase their level of support as they begin to develop a relationship with a school that provides them with opportunities to understand fully the school reform process. This evolving relationship leads the district to examine larger issues such as the nature of their role in this new environment where it is no longer adequate for them to function as they have in the past. At the same time, the school begins to view the district as partners and collaborators rather than inspectors and compliance monitors. A supportive school district is described by Levin (1993) as one that does the following:

• *Secures financial and human resources.* Supportive districts provide adequate release time for meetings, staff development, discussion, reflection, planning, and exploration; assist schools in the location of funding; and provide stability within the school by minimizing transfers and lay-offs.

• *Creates a safe environment for change.* Supportive districts foster a level of trust and are supportive of risk-taking. Each school site is given the responsibility of redistributing its resources to match its priorities; thus, by empowering the school to make decisions that were previously under the district's jurisdiction, the district enables the school to approach problems more creatively.

• *Builds awareness and support within the organization and reaching out to the community.* Supportive districts garner the support of state boards, community leaders, and unions by including them in the initial planning stages and encouraging their support and participation during implementation.

• *Provides technical and support services.* Supportive districts have the capacity to assist restructuring schools by providing information, technical assistance, staff development opportunities and expertise.

• *Creates network opportunities.* Districts, similar to state level organizations, are in an ideal position to help create networking opportunities for schools.

To enhance successful implementation of comprehensive school reform, school districts can build capacity through alignment and professional support systems (Meza, Teddlie, & Stringfield, 1998). The district's expectations and administrative procedures governing reform schools are aligned to support the school's priorities in the restructuring process. Areas of alignment include policies and reporting procedures, funding, and professional development.

The local school board, the central office, and the reform school work collaboratively to align state and district policy and to amend administrative regulations to support school improvement processes. One example of this collaborative effort is for the district to accept the comprehensive reform school improvement plan as the Title I school improvement plan, which is annually requested by the district and state. A second example of alignment is for the school district to consider how they select, assign, support, and evaluate principals (Levin, 1997).

Odden (1995) found that teaching all students to high standards is a goal that may not be achievable due to the way schools are fiscally managed. Through alignment, funding at the state and district level will be allocated to support the priorities established by the school improvement plans. One strategy the state and district can use is to cluster federal, state, and local financial resources, under the umbrella of school improvement and allocated in terms of school priorities. A second strategy is for the state, local school district, and school sites to reallocate existing funding, specifically those monies currently dedicated to non-instructional areas, to professional development and other school improvement priorities. Reallocation of funding is a strategy that may be particularly effective for many schools with high concentrations of students from low-income families.

Local school districts also align professional development for principals and teachers consistent with and focused on the priorities established by the schools. This professional alignment includes state level training, such as the Principal leadership training and workshops offered by the state's regional service centers. Professional development systems and networking build on the strengths of the diverse experiences of members of the comprehensive reform schools and provide revitalization to sustain the hard work of school change. District and statewide networking opportunities, such as grade level meetings, school visits, and periodic principal meetings, are offered to the schools. These professional meetings provide opportunities for collaborative work, directly tied to improved performance for students, with colleagues in the comprehensive reform network.

Some researchers indicate that, in support of school-based change, the district plays both a strategic and operational role. The central office must focus on providing a clear context and enabling resources such as time, funding, materials, and professional development, needed for school stakeholders to engage in the school reform process. This suggests a specific role for school boards: establishing student outcomes that are consistent with state mandates to guide school level improvement activities and district-level evaluations of progress. It also suggests a role for central administrators: organizing administrative structures and processes to support school-based change by providing a full range of enabling resources (Bauer, Meza, & Duplantis, 1999).

Conclusion

CSRD is a breakthrough that allows schools, districts and states to move beyond blame to real improvements in student learning and shared accountability. That does not mean implementing this reform strategy will be easy or always successful. Most difficult but rewarding efforts never are. Federal, state, and district educational policymakers, administrators, and teachers, supported by parents and community must continue to focus on what really counts: insisting on lasting academic outcomes for all children. Comprehensive school reform, when done well, combines the best of what research tells us works in the classroom, which also reflects what it takes to implement solid comprehensive school reform:

- Strong and supportive school, district, and state leadership;
- Improved and targeted professional development based on design implementation and school based priorities;
- Meaningful parental involvement;
- Teacher involvement and decision-making responsibility early in the process.
- Use of comprehensive school reform models with a proven track record of success.
- Alignment of instruction, curriculum, assessment, professional development, parental involvement, and school management to meet state standards and student outcomes.
- Buy-in and support from school faculty and district staff.
- Continuous evaluation of whether model is implemented correctly and what impact it is having on student learning and achievement.
- High quality external assistance from individuals experienced in comprehensive school reform.
- Thoughtful, good planning in matching the appropriate models to the needs of schools and students.

At its best, comprehensive school reform is an example of "top-down support for bottoms-up change" and shows promise for helping to rebuild schools by tapping the expertise of teachers, parents, principals, and district administrators. Incorporating this expertise with the help of experts who have studied, researched, and designed comprehensive school reform models based on what works offers hope – and increasingly a track record of success – for today's public schools. This will not happen, however, without meeting and rising above the "lessons learned" explored throughout this chapter.

Notes

1. This material was reprinted with permission from the Education Commission of the States in Denver, Co. , author of *Comprehensive School Reform: Five Lessons From the Field*, published in December, 1999.

References

Bauer, S., Meza, J., & Duplantis, M. (1999). Building conceptual model for shared accountability in an accelerated school district. Paper presented at the Annual Meeting of the American Educational Research Association, Montreal, Quebec, Canada.

Bodilly, S. (1998). *Lessons From New American Schools' Scale-up Phase*. Washington, D.C. RAND Education.

Buttram, J. L. (1999, July). Opening remarks for the Summer Institute on Comprehensive School Reform and Schoolwide Programs, Washington, D.C.

Cicchinelli, L. (1999). What we know about comprehensive school reform. *Noteworthy Perspectives on Comprehensive School Reform*. Mid-continent Regional Educational Laboratory.

Education Commission of the States (1998). *Comprehensive School Reform: Identifying Effective Models.*

Keltner, B. (1998). Funding Comprehensive School Reform. *Issue Paper*. Washington, D.C. RAND Education.

Levin, H. (1997). The dilemma of principal succession. *Accelerated Schools*, 6 (3): 1-17.

Levin, H. (1995). Making the decision to become an accelerated school. *Accelerated Schools*, 4 (2): 1-16.

Levin, H. (1993). Accelerating the system. *Accelerated Schools*, 3 (1): 1, 16-22.

Meza, J., Teddlie, C., & Stringfield, S. (1998). Tying school improvement to school accountablility: a review of the school effectiveness and assistance pilot study. Paper presented at the Annual Meeting of the American Educational Research Association, San Diego, California.

National CSRD Awards Database [Electronic database] (1999). Austin, TX: Southwest Educational Development Laboratory.

Odden, A. (1995). How to rethink school budgets to support school transformation. *New American Schools Getting Better by Design, 3*, New American Schools.

Southwest Educational Development Laboratory (January, 1999). Laboratory Support for Comprehensive School Reform. Austin, TX: Author.

U.S. Department of Education. (March, 1998). Guidance on the Comprehensive School Reform Demonstration Program. Washington, D.C.: Author.

CHAPTER 9

TOWARD MEETING THE AMERICAN DREAM: A FUTURE FOR TITLE I[1]

Sam Stringfield

We hold these truths to be self evident, that all men are created equal, that they are endowed by their creator with certain unalienable rights, that among these are Life, Liberty, and the pursuit of Happiness.

~Declaration of Independence

The first sentence of the second paragraph of the Declaration of Independence contains the essence of the meaning of the United States of America. From the Declaration through the Constitution, the Bill of Rights, and over 200 subsequent years of Constitutional Amendments and legislation, United States citizen's have debated and hammered out the meaning of the American Dream.

The author of those lines, Thomas Jefferson, dreamed of a nation of citizen farmers. As part of that dream he called for the unheard of: three years of free public education for every child who was to become a full voting citizen. Viewed from the twenty-first century, Jefferson's fervent hope seems pathetic. Only three years? Only for white males? But at the time Jefferson's dream was mocked for very different reasons. No nation had ever guaranteed a single year of free education to even that few of its citizens. In the eighteenth century, his dream of "universal" education was largely ignored in the United States. It was laughed at in the sophisticated capitals of Europe. On both hemi-

199

spheres, the idea that it was possible to teach, let alone that there might be value in teaching, the great unwashed masses to read was viewed as a romantic dream.

By the middle of the twentieth century, the United States had not only met but greatly exceeded Jefferson's original dream. Public education was a right for literally all children. In most states attending school was a mandated obligation of all students through at least age 16. In theory, every state guaranteed the right to a free public education through high school.

Over the last 200 years, other relatively developed nations have followed America's lead in providing a free and public education. However, perhaps because they were able to observe our mistakes, virtually all other nations chose methods for funding schools that did not rely (as had the US) on local land taxes. The effect is paradoxical in that by the 1950s virtually every developed nation had evolved a system of support for the education for all children that would not discriminate against children of poverty. In the Netherlands, for example, a school is funded on a national, per-student basis, with two exceptions. A child of poverty is funded at 1.25 times the rate of a middle-class child, and a child whose parents speak a language other than Dutch is funded at 1.90.

Lyndon Johnson may not have been aware of the international educational comparisons when he became president of the United States; however, as a young man Johnson had briefly been a teacher of poor children in a rural, Texas, one-room, school-house. There was, and remains, a palpable anger among teachers in under-funded schools and districts as they observe their talented poor children hitting a series of hard and unmoving ceilings. Johnson clearly came to know and be offended by the grotesque funding inequalities in his native state which resulted in his young charges having pitifully fewer educational opportunities than the children of their more affluent neighbors, only a few miles away.

Decades later, as president of the United States, Lyndon Johnson drove the 1965 Elementary and Secondary Education Act (ESEA) through Congress (see Kemper & Taylor, Chapter 2). For the first year of this remarkable bill, Johnson asked for funding of just over $1 billion, and received funding of just under $1 billion. The next year he asked for over $2 billion, and received barely half that amount. From 1965 through 2000, Title I has never been fully funded for a single year. In spite of this, for over a third of a century Title I has been the one national attempt to make educational funding in the United States more equitable.

Several facts make Title I's role very important historically as well as currently. From the end of World War II until today, the economic effect of obtaining an adequate education has been on the rise. In the late 1940s, for example, a young American adult male, age 25-34, who dropped out of high school would, on average, make 80% as much per year as a similarly aged male who had graduated from college. By the mid-1970s, a similar drop-out could expect to make about two thirds as much as a young college graduate. But by 1998, U.S. census data indicated that a 25-34 year old American male high school drop out was making, on average, less than half as much the drop-out from the 1970s (in inflation-adjusted dollars), and about one-third of what a similarly aged college graduate was making. Across two generations, the differential had expanded from 20% to over 200%. As we have moved from a modern, industrialized national economy to a post-modern, global information economy, the effect on both individuals and nations of having anything other that first-quality educational opportunities for all young people has become close to disastrous.

As Borman's meta-analysis in Chapter 2 of this volume illustrates (see also Borman, Stringfield, and Slavin, in press), Title I has produced positive achievement gains in both reading and mathematics. Contributing less than 5% of the nation's expenditures on K-12 education, Title I's effect has stabilized at a national average effect size of +.15. That's a quite respectable return on what is, in the larger context, a very modest additional investment.

There are many well-documented instances where Title I's effects have been much greater. From case studies (see *Journal of Education for Students Placed At Risk*, Volumes 1-5 for many examples) to large national studies (e.g., Stringfield et al., 1997; Slavin, Karweit, & Madden, 1989; Slavin & Fashola, 1998) paths are being opened to evermore effective uses of our Nation's modest investment. In analyzing longitudinal data from the National Assessment of Educational Progress (NAEP), Grissmer, Flanagan, Kawata, & Williamson (2000) make a strong case that money carefully targeted at improving the resources available to, and working conditions of, teachers of high poverty students can result in average gains of at least 15 percentile points for those high-poverty students. Grissmer (2000) estimates that a tripling of carefully targeted Title I expenditure would yield significantly increased returns on investments.

It follows that the future of Title I should be very bright. There is a clear national interest in having all young Americans having a shot at the American Dream. There is clear evidence that Title I has both an overall effect and a very substantial effect in "best practice" locations. The remainder of this chapter is dedicated to exploring available methods for greatly increasingly the effects of Title I.

Building a Continuously Improving, Highly Reliable Title I

What would it take to make Title I more effective over the long haul? Three things: (1) clarify goals and measures, (2) vigorously support local moves to best practice, and (3) dramatically increase funding.

Clarify Goals and Measures

Jennings (in press) and McDill and Natriello (in press) make it clear that goals of Title I have shifted awkwardly over the program's 35-year history. Both the Congress and the US Department of Education have shied away from specifying goals and measures.

Goals have shifted over time, from the simple provision of additional resources to whole districts, to the provision of money targeted to high poverty schools, to having students in those schools show academic gains. Measures have shifted even more frequently, from essentially no accountability, pre-post measures on norm-referenced tests (the TIERS system, Tallmadge and Wood, 1982), to allegedly clear, systemic measures with no requirement for measurement at all until state mandated testing programs come on line. By contrast, research on Highly Reliable Organizations (Roberts, 1990, 1993; Stringfield, 1995) has repeatedly found that to be effective, highly reliable organizations have a few, sacrosanct goals, which are addressed in a data/information-rich environment.

The Congress and the Department of Education must make crystal clear that Title I exists to improve the reading and mathematics skills of students who, by virtue of historical disadvantage, have been placed at risk of academic failure. The rich databases relevant to those goals must be available to participants at all levels.

The next necessary goal is to re-implement and improve a system of clear measures of the desired goals. The measures should be clear, and related to the limited, focused, goals of the program have defensible psychometric properties, and reasonable face-validity. The measures should be "value added" (e.g., longitudinal gain), not point in time. The measures have to be broad enough to be worth "teaching to the test" (Slavin, in press).

To the best of this author's knowledge, there is not a single state that meets those criteria today. As three examples, California has elegant "frameworks," but uses a traditional, nationally standardized, narrow, norm-referenced test as its measure of achievement. Texas has a very narrow state-produced test, and Maryland uses a series of tests that are only administered in three grades. None of Maryland's measures provides student-level "value added" and none is of debatable psychometric sturdiness.

Given the perhaps impossibly high hurdles that would have to be crossed to achieve national tests and testing for Title I, the federal government will have to accelerate it's push for high-quality, state-level goal setting and concrete measurement. To date the federal government has shown almost no willingness to push states in this "mandated" direction. For Title I to become more effective, the federal government is going to have to establish consequences for states that avoid legislated mandates to establish and measure clear goals.

Vigorously Supporting Local Moves to Best Practice

Second, to gain further improvements in Title I effects, the federal government is going to have to greatly expand its activities around the creation and dissemination of proven whole school reforms.

The existing research is reasonably clear that engaging a whole school in a unified change effort is generally more effective than changing a sub-component of the school and assuming others will adapt (Stringfield et al., 1997; Nunnery, 1998). The same studies and reviews of research have found that, in general, partnering with an external reform design is more likely to be productive than efforts to "home brew" change.

Supporting the ongoing creation of new whole-school reform can be a central role for the federal government. An often-overlooked fact about the Success For All program (Slavin et al., 1996) is that while in development, the program received years of moderate-but-stable funding through the (former) Center for Research on Effective Schooling for Disadvantaged Students, and the current Center for Research on the Education of Students Placed At Risk, both funded by the U.S. Office of Educational Research and Improvement. The stability and long-term nature of the funding were probably as important as the total number of dollars. Somewhat similarly, five-year funding was provided to the New American Schools designs (see Stringfield, Ross, & Smith, 1996), although the funding was private.

A related federal contribution would be support for a series of large-scale, multi-year evaluations of diverse school reform designs. Herman et al. (1999) reviewed research on 25 such designs. While the authors found some research on most of these self-proclaimed "research-based" designs, they also expressed the hope that much, much more research would follow. As a practical matter, private foundations are much more inclined to support development and implementation projects than longitudinal, third party evaluations. Thus, the task must fall to the federal government.

Having funded the development and third party evaluation of promising programs, Title I should greatly expand its Comprehensive School Reform Demonstration (CSRD) program (see Meza, et al., Chapter 8). At present, CSRD is funded at $150 million per year, and supports approximately 2500 schools in their reform efforts. As research on which of the 150+ reform designs produce greater effects emerges, Title I should increase funding for CSRD, and encourage targeting funding towards the more effective designs.

However, in practice as in research, reliability sets the upper boundary of validity. The most "valid" program can have zero effect if poorly implemented (for clear examples, see Stringfield et al., 1997; Stringfield, 1999). Summarizing 16 studies conducted by the Center for Social Organization of Schools during the 1990's, Datnow and Stringfield (2000) concluded that reliable school reform had several characteristics, regardless of the specific reform attempted. Those common characteristics can be summarized as follows:

- The full faculty, the school's and the district's administration must become clear on a specific set of shared goals. Those goals must be tied to a long-term, whole-team focus on key measures of school improvement.

- Districts need a coordinated and broad-based plan for disseminating information about reform options.
- Each school must engage in a thoughtful, critical process of inquiry about their students' and faculty's current needs, and the steps needed to meet shared goals. This must precede the selection of any reform design or strategy. Good decisions about reform take time.
- Reform designs and reform designers must view local context and the diversity of languages, races, classes, and genders of those involved as strengths to build on. The developers, whether local or national, must see teachers as an asset and as collaborators, not simply as implementers of reform. From the first day forward, the reform must affect the whole school, not just be a "pocket program." The reform must address technical, normative, and political dimensions of change; and it must include equity as an explicit goal.
- The design team, the district, and the school's administration must work together to provide multidimensional, ongoing support and leadership.
- Policy systems must be aligned to support the specific reform that is ongoing at each school.
- Successful implementation requires sensitivity and adaptability without academic compromise. The combination of sensitivity and adaptability are required of the design developers, the state/local policy makers, and educators in schools. States, districts, and design teams must be willing to change along with schools. Such active, shared growth is at the heart of both co-construction and high reliability.

Dramatically Increasing Title I Funding

Increases in CSRD could, in theory, come from simply decreasing the remainder of Title I; however, research by Hedges, Laine, and Greenwald (1994), and Payne and Biddle (1999) clearly demonstrate that carefully targeted additions to total educational funding can make a substantial difference. Payne and Biddle's work is particularly clear in demonstrating the deleterious effects of disproportionate under-funding of schools and school districts serving poor children. Given that Title I is the one national antidote to under-funding poor children's schools and districts, Grissmer (2000) estimates that a tripling of the total size of Title I, accompanied with careful targeting of the new resources, would produce a gain of as much as 15 national percentage points for America's children of poverty. That would be a very real gain at a readily achievable cost.

Summary

America is rapidly moving into a global information economy. Achieving a high level of academic attainment for all citizens is a critical national goal in such a worldwide economic environment. For over a third of a century, Title I has been the United States largest, national, educational investment to allow all citizens access to the American Dream. Diverse studies and meta-analyses have documented Title I's successes. Still, the program can and must improve if our nation is to achieve its goals.

Three steps can be taken to increase the effectiveness of Title I. First, Congress, the Department of Education, and the fifty states can make the goals and measures for Title I completely clear and cogent. Second, Title I can vigorously support national development of and local moves toward best practice. Congress can fund the aggressive development and independent testing of new interventions for at risk students. Congress can then fund, and the US Department of Education can work with the states, to support dissemination of those practices. A good deal of research already exists on how to move from design to implementation to institutionalization, and more is needed. Third, the president and the Congress can dramatically increase Title I funding.

Each one of the millions of at risk children in the United States of America deserves a chance at the American Dream. A continuously improving, reliable Title I has been and can be an invaluable tool in guaranteeing that all children have a fair shot at that dream.

Notes

1. Support for this study was provided by a grant from the Office of Educational Research and Improvement, U.S. Department of Education (Grant No. $117D-40005) to the Center for Research on the Education of Students Placed At Risk (CRESPAR). However, any opinions expressed by the author are his own, and do not represent the policies or positions of the US Department of Education.

2. By the mid-1990s only two developed countries relied heavily on local land taxes for the support of public schools: the U.S.A. and South Africa.

3. The field of comparative education was in its infancy, and such now-widely-discussed international comparative studies of education as TIMSS had not yet been imagined in 1965.

4. See Reich (1992), Deming (1993) and Friedman (1999) for a discussion of the importance of education to individuals and nations in a world economy.

5. As an example, from the summer of 1999, the State of Colorado's Title I office had not targeted a single Title I school as needing improvement in over five years.

6. A few years ago, this author was involved in a study that included some Texas elementary schools. As part of the study, we administered the Comprehensive Test of Basic Skills, 4th Edition (CTB/McGraw-Hill, 1989) to several classrooms of students in several grades in three Texas elementary schools. The test is no longer sold by CTB, in part because CTB researchers believe that their current, 5th edition does a much better job of measuring "higher order" content. Yet several Texas teachers observed to me that they thought that CTBS/4 was much more "higher order" than TAAS, the state-mandated Texas achievement test.

7. Nunnery (1998) concludes that the reason for this is that local development of a design typically takes a full year and expends the local developers' energy for reform. Hence, the majority of locally developed designs simply never get to the classrooms.

References

Borman (this volume). *The overall effectiveness of Title I: A review of recent research.*

Borman, G., & D'Agostino, J. (in press). Title I and student achievement: A quantitative synthesis. In G. Borman, S. Stringfield, and R. Slavin, R. (eds.), *Title I: Compensatory education at the crossroads.* Mahwah, NJ: Erlbaum.

Borman, G., Stringfield, S., & Slavin, R. (in press). *Title I: Compensatory education at the crossroads.* Mahwah, NJ: Erlbaum.

CTB/Macmillan/McGraw-Hill (1989). *The Comprehensive Test of Basic Skills.* Monterey, CA: CTB/Macmillan/McGraw-Hill.

Datnow, A., & Stringfield, S. (2000). Working together for reliable school reform. *Journal of Education for Students Placed At Risk, 5* (1 & 2), 183-204.

Deming, W. E. (1993). *The new economics for industry, government, education.* Cambridge, MA: MIT.

Friedman, T. L. (1999). *The Lexus and the olive tree.* New York: Farrar, Straus, and Giroux.

Grabbard, D. A. (ed.) (2000). *Knowledge and power in the global economy.* Mahwah, NJ: Erlbaum.

Grissmer, D. (May, 2000). Personal Communication.

Grissmer, D., Flanagan, A., Kawata, J., & Williamson, S. (2000). Improving student achievement: *What state NAEP test scores tell us.* Santa Monica, CA: Rand.

Herman, R., Aladjem, D., McMahon, P., Masem, E., Mulligan, I., O'Malley, A., Quinones, S., Reeve, A., & Woodruff, D. (1999). *An educator's guide to schoolwide reform.* Washington, DC: American Institutes for Research.

Jennings, J. (in press). Title I: Its legislative history and its promise. In G. Borman, S. Stringfield, and R. Slavin, R. (eds.), *Title I: Compensatory education at the crossroads.* Mahwah, NJ: Erlbaum.

Reich, R.B. (1992). *The work of nations.* New York: Random House.

Roberts, C. (1990). Some characteristics of high reliability organizations. *Organizational Science, 1* (2), 1-17.

Roberts, K. (1993). *New challenges to understanding organizations.* New York: Macmillan

Slavin, R., & Fashola, O. (1998). *Show me the evidence!* Thousand Oaks, CA: Corwin.

Slavin, R. (in press). How Title I can become the engine of reform in America's schools. In G. Borman, S. Stringfield, and

R. Slavin, R. (eds.), *Title I: Compensatory education at the crossroads*. Mahwah, NJ: Erlbaum.

Slavin, R.E., Madden, N.A., Dolan, L.J., Wasik, B.A., Ross, S., Smith, L., & Dianda, M. (1996). Success for All: A summary of research. *Journal of Education for Students Placed At Risk, 1* (1), 41-76.

Slavin, R.E., Karweit, N.L., & Madden, N.A. (Eds.) (1989). *Effective programs for students at risk.* Boston: Allyn and Bacon.

Stringfield, S., Billig, S., & Davis, A. (1991). Chapter 1 program improvement: Cause for cautious optimism and a call for much more research. *Educational Evaluation and Policy Analysis, 13*(4), 399-406.

Stringfield, S. (1995). Attempts to enhance students' learning: A search for valid programs and highly reliable implementation techniques. *School Effectiveness and School Improvement.* 6(1), 67-96.

Stringfield, S. (1999). The phoenix rises from its ashes. . . doesn't it? In J. Freiberg (Ed.), *School Climate: Measuring, improving and sustaining healthy learning environments* (pp. 186-207). London: Falmer.

Stringfield, S., Millsap, M.A., Herman, R., Yoder, N., Brigham, N., Nesselrodt, P., Schaffer, E., Karweit, N., Levin, M., & Stevens, R. (1997). *Urban and suburban/rural special strategies for educating disadvantaged children. Final report.* Washington, DC: U.S. Department of Education.

Stringfield, S., Ross, S., & Smith, L. (Eds.). (1996). *Bold plans for school restructuring: The New American Schools designs.* Mahwah, NJ: Erlbaum.

Tallmadge, G.K., & Wood, C.T. (1982). *User's guide to the ESEA Title I evaluation and reporting system.* Mountain View, CA: RMC Research Corporation.

CHAPTER 10

SORTING THROUGH THE EVIDENCE: POLICY IMPLICATIONS FOR TITLE I SCHOOLWIDE PROGRAMS

Dianne L. Taylor & Elizabeth A. Kemper

The chapters in this volume provide a vantage point for understanding the evolution of the Title I program over its 35-year history from inception to the current focus on the schoolwide and Comprehensive School Reform Demonstration (CSRD) programs. From this vantage point, the reader is offered empirical evidence regarding the impact of federal, state, and district policies on the success of Title I in general, and schoolwide programs in particular. In this concluding chapter of the book, we examine both the harmful and helpful effects of past policy, and draw together recommendations from across the chapters for future policy. Interestingly, as we conducted this examination, we found that the most important themes in the volume were not emphasized in the research on Title I programs, but are consistent with themes from research on school improvement.

Good Intentions, Unintended Results

The central thrust of ESEA and of Title I was to eliminate poverty by improving the quality of education available to poor children. President Johnson's successful expansion of the federal government into the arena of public education enabled policy-makers in Washington to promulgate laws and regulations unencumbered by local prejudices and predilections. Thus, it is ironic that in spite of the altruistic goal of helping economically

211

disadvantaged students, federal policies have more often served to undermine actual programmatic implementation than to support it.

Policy Instability

Practitioners affected by Title I have seen several shifts in emphasis over the past 35 years, sometimes driven by political philosophy (see Kemper & Taylor, Chapter 1) rather than by a commitment to improve educational services for the indigent. Although a well-established theme in the school improvement literature is the difficulty of using policy as the lever for changing teaching practices at the classroom level, the model used to provide educational services has been at the heart of policy instability.

In the 1970s, Title I changed from a non-prescriptive policy allocating funds to districts, to a punitive policy focused on monitoring federal funds. Penalties for "misspending" Title I dollars were so onerous that districts opted for pullout programs that could pass the scrutinizing eye of federal auditors. As pointed out in several chapters in this book, federal monitoring concentrated on dollars, not on improving educational outcomes for disadvantaged children.

For Title I, in any of its iterations, to improve the educational achievement of disadvantaged children implicitly requires changing teaching practice. Unwittingly, the federal policy that resulted in widespread use of the pullout model appears to have worked at cross-purposes with changing practice, despite mounting evidence over the life of the Title I program that a variety of teaching practices effectively engage children in learning.

Pullout programs obviated any need for regular classroom teachers to change teaching practices. Students who were pulled out received extra assistance and traditional strategies enabled students who were not pulled out to maintain acceptable levels of achievement. The assumption that traditional strategies were effective was not only supported by this logic, but also by teachers' diminished sense of responsibility for the achievement of students who were pulled out. As Angelle (Chapter 3) reports, regular classroom teachers abdicated responsibility for the achievement of "Title I students" in proportion to the amount of time these students were taught in the pullout setting. Though Title I pullout programs consistently failed to eliminate the achievement gap between middle class and economically deprived children (see

Borman, Chapter 2), pullout became so ingrained as the delivery model that practitioners are continuing to use it today, notwithstanding a school's ostensible participation in a schoolwide program (see Ceperley, Chapter 6).

Federal mistrust of local districts, however well-founded, supplanted the goal of eliminating poverty through education. Tracing dollars rather than adopting and using effective teaching strategies became the de facto goal of Title I policy. In an effort to redirect attention to the goal of improving the achievement of low-income youngsters, the Hawkins-Stafford Amendments of 1988 permitted, and the Improving America's Schools Act of 1994 encouraged, schoolwide programs. In addition, the Obey-Porter legislation of 1997 encouraged and funded the use of various special strategies (see Meza, Dahlkemper, & Buttram, Chapter 8).

These amendments represent another radical change in federal policy and were initially slow to catch on. One reason districts shied away from the schoolwide option was the restrictive thresholds for eligibility, laid out in the Hawkins-Stafford Amendments, that schools were required to satisfy before they were allowed to implement schoolwide programs. As the eligibility restrictions were relaxed, stringent accountability requirements for student achievement on standardized tests were added. Though schools have adopted schoolwide programs in great numbers since 1994, evidence presented across chapters in this book suggests that the emphasis on test scores is now supplanting the adoption and use of effective teaching practices that would improve student learning.

The Effects of High Stakes Testing
The current focus on state mandated testing programs, reinforced by federal law, appears to be hampering development of strong schoolwide Title I programs. If schools must comply with state and district directives regarding state testing programs, little room is left for adopting a schoolwide plan that meets the needs of individual students.

The four chapters that form Part II of this book present case study research in twelve schools implementing schoolwide plans. Two of these chapters focus on schools at which schoolwide plans were implemented with some success; the other two chapters describe schools at which implementation was unsuccessful. The studies reported by these authors included observations in classrooms at the respective schools. These observations revealed that traditional teaching techniques were found across classrooms and schools, though teachers at schools successfully implementing plans tended to use the strategies more effectively than their counterparts at the other schools. Interestingly, traditional techniques prevailed even at a school successfully implementing one of the "special strategies," Success for All, as part of its schoolwide plan.

The twelve schools described in Part II are located in four districts that are in four states. We note this because state and local policies differ from district to district and state to state. This said, one policy was common across these schools and their respective districts and states, an emphasis on statewide norm- and criterion-referenced testing programs as the prime determinant of school success. The burden of the testing programs was particularly problematic at a school studied by Wong and Alkins (Chapter 5) at which teachers noted that the school's vision "was passing the state tests" (p. 111). At schools studied by Taylor and Teddlie (Chapter 4), teachers were similarly aware of the importance of test results. One teacher noted, "'I am not certain how [the Title I program] affects test scores, but I have seen big improvements in the work and attitudes of students.'" Unfortunately, "big improvements" in students' work and attitudes were believed by teachers at this school to be secondary to test results.

If teaching techniques are to change, policies at all levels – federal, state, district, and school – need to change so that multiple indicators of effectiveness are considered, including data about the quality of the schoolwide plan, a schoolwide emphasis on effective teaching strategies, and on-going, job-embedded professional development that involves teachers and principals. As Meza, Dahlkemper, and Buttram (Chapter 8) recommend, policies that foster school improvement at the level of classroom teaching practices are needed to prevent a continuation of the mediocre achievement that Borman (Chapter 2) describes.

Factors Promoting Program Success

Program and Funding Allocation Flexibility
An important finding in this book is the importance of flexibility extended to schools in both designing schoolwide programs and allocating resources to support them. The impor-

tance of flexibility is not a new theme in the school improvement literature; Hallinger and Murphy raised the issue in 1986. However, the use of flexibility as a support for improvement efforts is often overlooked. Wong and Alkins (Chapter 5) describe latitude in fashioning schoolwide plans accorded to schools by the respective districts. The districts involved in their research had promulgated improvement programs with specific attributes. Nonetheless, individual schoolwide plans were allowed to vary provided they remained consistent with the districts' overall school improvement goals. Taylor and Teddlie (Chapter 4) also discuss district level flexibility, noting that one school was allowed to implement its own improvement strategies, while another school was able to adopt a special strategy. In all of these cases, implementation of the schoolwide plans was relatively successful.

Flexibility is also important in allocating resources. In addition to devolving programmatic decisions to the school level, the districts that Wong and Alkins studied also combined Title I and other available resources to increase the number of teacher assistants to schools with high percentages of children for whom English was not their first language. Coordinating resources does not make up for other problems at the school, however. Ceperley (Chapter 6) describes an innovative strategy for coordinating Title I monies with state, district, and local funds to maintain, at least partially, early childhood programs at several schools. In the absence of effective leadership, however, the coordination of resources did not result in programmatic innovation nor in the adoption of research-proven instructional strategies at the school she studied.

School Leadership

The flexibility discussed above, while important, is not sufficient for schoolwide plans to be successfully implemented. Strong, effective leadership is essential, as Meza, Dahlkemper, and Buttram (Chapter 8) point out. In several chapters, authors conclude that the leadership abilities of the principals account, at least in part, for differences in implementation success. Where principals were strong leaders, schools more fully implemented the schoolwide plan. Where leadership was weak, schoolwide plans tended to be implemented poorly. For example, the principal of the school Ceperley (Chapter 6) studied was well liked by parents, who found him accessible. Nonetheless, the principal undermined the potential effectiveness of the schoolwide plan by maintaining a hands-off stance toward the instructional program, steering clear of classroom visits, providing time but not guidance for collaborative planning, and frequently interrupting instructional time with announcements that were not pressing. At this school, there was no apparent urgency about student learning, nor any sense that merely intensifying traditional teaching practices was inadequate for improving the education and learning of the students.

The importance of principal leadership emerges in a different and intriguing way in both Chapter 4 and Chapter 7. Taylor and Teddlie (Chapter 4) compare two schools that were successfully implementing their schoolwide plans. They note that leadership differences resulted in more effective implementation at one school than at the other. Although the schools served similar populations, the stronger leader worked with the faculty to fashion a plan specific to needs at the school and garnered support from the faculty for implementation. The weaker principal opted to implement a special strategy and failed to procure faculty buy-in, leading to variations in effectiveness at the classroom level.

McCoy and Mencer (Chapter 7) also compare two schools, though these schools were unsuccessful in implementing the schoolwide plan. These authors describe numerous inadequacies at both schools; however, they conclude by noting their greater optimism about one school than the other. The difference was the leadership ability of the principal. The school about which McCoy and Mencer were hopeful had a principal who, though new to the school, was enthusiastic about the schoolwide plan, participated with teachers during instructional planning, and taught demonstration lessons. Her leadership style is a stark contrast to that of the principal described by Ceperley.

Schools attended by low-income children in impoverished neighborhoods are rarely seen as desirable assignments by principals. Instead what often happens is that these schools are led by principals who were unsuccessful elsewhere, or who prove to be weak leaders. In light of the nationwide principal shortage, this practice is unlikely to change. Nonetheless, the findings reported in these chapters suggest that districts implementing schoolwide programs should pursue a policy that assures the most capable principals are placed at the schools with Title I programs.

Recommendations for Increasing Title I Effectiveness

Authors of the chapters in this volume make a number of useful recommendations for future policy. We will address a few of the recurrent recommendations here.

Professional Development

High quality professional development that is targeted to priorities identified at a school and included in the schoolwide plan is essential if school improvement efforts are to succeed (see Meza et al., Chapter 8). Piecemeal efforts and/or requiring teachers to spend hours being told about the newest policies issued by the state or district will not bring about the needed changes at the school or classroom level. Ceperley (Chapter 6) makes this point by arguing that including professional development as a component of the schoolwide plan does not ensure that the school adopts a schoolwide approach to professional development.

Professional development must be tightly linked in a coherent manner to the goals and objectives of the schoolwide plan. Simply allocating dollars and leaving teachers to their own discretion in seeking out professional development will not build capacity at the school. Coaches of athletic teams understand the importance of building organizational capacity, but this lesson is seldom reflected in schoolwide plans. Unfortunately, it appears that teachers at the most impoverished schools have the fewest opportunities for professional development (see Borman, Chapter 2). At the same time, Borman reports that on-going professional development is linked to a greater likelihood that more engaging instructional strategies will be adopted and used.

Leadership and Support

The importance of school-based leadership was discussed extensively above. Not discussed was the importance of leadership at all levels, including district, state, and federal. Nor was the type of leadership discussed. Abundant research on transformational leadership indicates that school improvement is more likely to flow from facilitative leadership than from leadership exercised in an authoritarian manner. Moreover, the evidence from Title I research is clear that the coercive characteristics of the old pullout model did not eliminate the achievement gap between middle class and disadvantaged children, though this was the goal.

Leadership can and should function as a resource and a support for school based efforts. Stringfield (Chapter 9) and Meza and his colleagues (Chapter 8) draw attention to the importance of leadership efforts at the district, and we would add the state, level in assisting schools in a number of ways. One of the most important is conducting a thoughtful school assessment that critically examines the strengths and weaknesses of the professional staff and student body. A great deal of sensitivity is needed to support school efforts in this regard, but district and state leaders can make an enormous contribution by offering that sensitivity coupled with guidance.

Conducting a school assessment is only the initial step, however. Schools are in need of external expertise that can be provided by the district and state. Such experts can help with the development of improvement plans that are cohesive and coherent. The school studied by Ceperley was hampered in its improvement efforts by making poor program choices; schools studied by Wong and Alkins could only implement one or two components of their plans at a time; schools studied by Taylor and Teddlie and by McCoy and Mencer were compromised in their improvement efforts by having too many plan components. Guidance provided by external leaders can assist schools in fashioning improvement plans that have tight internal links among identified needs, goals, objectives, and outcomes.

Districts and state leaders can also provide support by making available much needed resources. Money is only one resource needed, and may not be the most important. Other resources such as time, expertise, and support for risk-taking may lead schools to create innovative options that maximize monetary expenditures, such as sharing a reading expert among several neighboring schools. Additionally, districts and states can provide support by consolidating the guidelines for improvement plans at the school level so that one plan serves needs at the three levels.

Teacher Involvement
A third recommendation, and one that is intertwined with leadership, is to involve teachers in the decision making about the schoolwide program. The history of school reform over the past 30 years indicates that teachers are unlikely to be willing implementers of reforms developed elsewhere. Teachers need to work in conjunction with administrators at the school and district level

to fashion a schoolwide plan for improvement that includes everyone's voice. Involving teachers in developing the plan sets a foundation for them to increase their commitment and sense of responsibility for plan implementation and results. Excluding teachers or involving them marginally can result in limited teacher buy-in.

Teachers were very involved in developing the schoolwide plan at one of the schools studied by Taylor and Teddlie (Chapter 4), but were only marginally involved at the other school, which was implementing a special strategy. Although differences in the leadership capacity of the principals at the two schools likely accounted for the degree to which teachers were involved in decision making, it should be noted that at the school where teachers' input was lower, so was their support for the special strategy.

Matching Methods and Models to Schools

A flurry of interest has accompanied the Obey-Porter legislation funding CSRD programs. We caution, however, that neither the selection of a "special strategy" nor the development of a "home grown" improvement strategy is a silver bullet. School improvement is difficult work that exacts a price in time and energy from teachers and administrators. The path taken for school improvement should be that indicated by the results of a comprehensive assessment of school needs.

As part of the needs assessment, the faculty and administrative staff, with the assistance of district and state leaders, need to examine the research on the strengths and weaknesses of models included in the CSRD legislation, as well as research on methods that can be used independently of models. The degree of success of "research-proven" models and methods depends on the commitment of the teachers (see Chapter 4). The model or method notwithstanding, a faculty of highly committed teachers will lead to success. Two decades of effective schools research bear this out. Conversely, when faculty are unsupportive of a model or method, little improvement will be forthcoming regardless of success stories elsewhere. Three decades of research on school reform bear this out.

Matching a reform to a school means understanding not only the unique contextual elements of the school, but also the unique requirements and elements of the reform model or method. This matching process necessarily entails building faculty and adminis-trator support for the procedure adopted.

After 35 years, Title I still holds promise for improving schools. The recommendations made in this chapter and through-out the book can serve states, districts, and schools well in their pursuit of strong learning outcomes for low-income children.